The Adventurer's Journal

Selina Belle

www.inomniaparatuspublishing.com

Very special thank yous

To my publisher for supporting me through this ever-expanding creative journey and being my guide.

Giarc, Kim, and Lisa, thank you for being the best friends an Adventurer could ask for. For the moral support, proofreading, brainstorming, and all the other -ings that came with getting this journal ready. I couldn't have done it without you.

And to the Adventurers who use this journal to better their lives, thank you for letting me be part of your journey.

Happy Questing!

- Selina Belle

Welcome Adventurer

Welcome to this magical world where fantasy and reality mix, and you, Adventurer, travel on an exciting journey. Here the Quests are real. The rewards are real. And the positive impacts each Quest makes on your life are real. The world you create within this journal straddles both worlds of fantasy and reality. Magically designed to help you achieve your dreams and desires in the real world while exploring the magical world within.

If you are new to this world, I encourage you to add the Tome of Achievement to your Journey. It will greatly enhance your use of this journal. The Tome of Achievement is magical and created this journal as a companion so that the journey you started there can continue on here.

The Tome of Achievement guides you through every step of creating the epic Quests and ensures you are properly prepared with everything and everyone you need to be successful. Designing your Quest has never been easier, and completing it has never been so much fun!

The Adventurer's Journal has all the critical elements of Quest tracking and journaling laid out for you in the Tome of Achievement so you may record your journey for future generations. Or to refer back to when you need to be reminded of how you defeated a monster. (Did I mention we straddle fantasy and reality here?)

Quests are goals. Monsters are challenges. And Rewards are real. Welcome back Adventurer to this magical world. Your amazing future awaits!

Happy Questing!

- *Selina Belle*

.

Imagine
a world where
you are an
adventurer and
the Quest you
embark on has
the potential to
change your life!

Welcome to that
world Adventurer!
You have stepped
into the first day
of a new exciting
adventure!

- Selina Belle

Codex of Terms

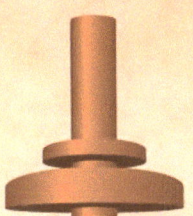 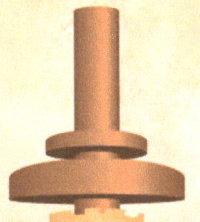

Adventurer,

If you are new to adventuring, this Codex of Terms will become very useful to you.

Part of the magic held in this book includes a formula to take ordinary goals and goal-setting and turn them into extraordinary quests.

Remember to reference this page regularly.

Happy Questing!
Selina Belle

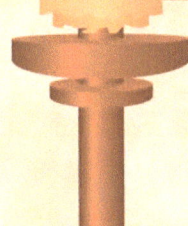 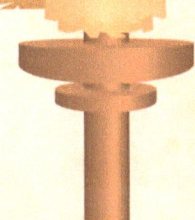

Codex of Terms (Glossary)

A list of important terms needed to utilize this tome to the fullest.

Tome

A guidebook. It's magical, so we called it a tome. Grimoire seemed a little too over the top.

Journal

A companion to a Tome where you track your progress, record your thoughts and record your journey.

Parchment

The paper this tome is written on. (Use your imagination. Real parchment is made of untanned animal skins. This is just paper that looks like parchment. Work with me here!)

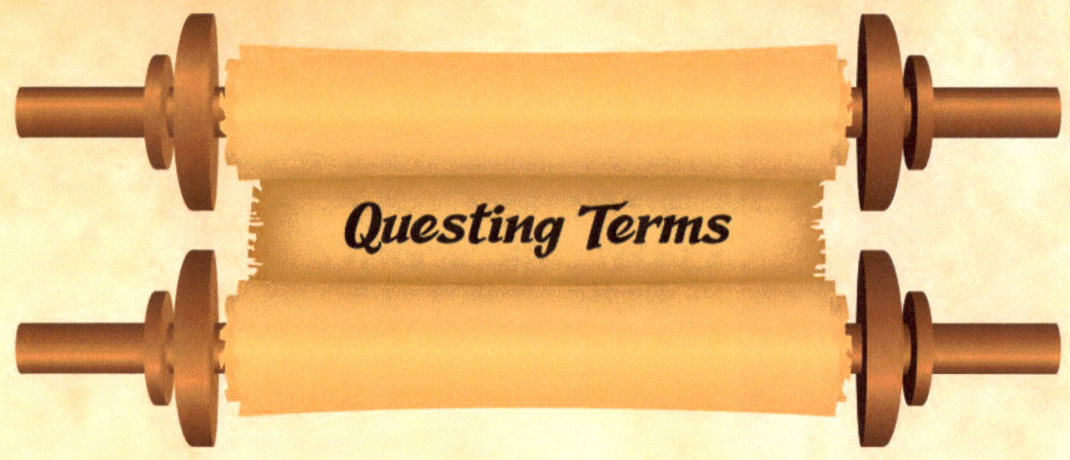

Quests & Goals

Quests (Goals)

A goal is when an adventurer or adventurers have a vision for a future achievement and put significant effort towards achieving it.

Main Quest (Primary Goal)

The Main Quest is the Quest (goal) an adventurer chooses to focus on. These Quests tend to take months to complete and should make significant progress toward achieving a better future for the adventurer in some way. Main Quests usually have several Sub-Quests that need to be completed as part of it.

Sub-Quests (Milestones)

Sub-Quests are large projects or achievements that need to be completed in order to make progress in the Main Quest. Sub-Quests usually have several steps or tasks that need to be completed as part of it.

Side Quests

Side Quests are projects, tasks and to-do items that don't have anything to do with the Main Quest or its Sub-Quests but still need to be accomplished. These can take several weeks or a few minutes depending on the Side Quest.

Tasks (To-Do Items)

Tasks are to-do items that must be accomplished to complete a Sub-Quest or Side Quest. These usually only take a few minutes, or at most a few hours. Rewards for Tasks are received as TP in the Daily Stats Log's Reward Center.

Resources

Allies

People who are there to support you. They provide you with feedback, moral support and sounding boards. They are the ones who help you when you are feeling down or want to celebrate success. Allies often show up as coaches, trainers, teachers, friends, and family members.

Party Members

Specialists in their field, party members help you with completing special tasks. They may have a skill you don't possess, or they are someone you can delegate to. They travel the Quest with you and share in the successes, sub-quests, and battles. Party Members often show up as employees, contractors, bards, warriors, archers, familiars, horses, etc.

Other Resources

Tools, equipment, money, and knowledge repositories that may be helpful during your Quest.

Rewards & Treasure

Rewards & Treasure Chests

While Questing, you will earn ways to get Treasure Chests! Rewards are the items or gifts you give yourself when you earn a treasure chest. There are several different levels of treasure chests you will learn about when you reach the Treasure Room. It's important to note that gifts do not have to be financial in nature. A gift of time is often more powerful and valuable to your well-being than that ice cream sundae with extra fudge and... ah hem... I digress.

Treasure Points (TP)

Points you earn as you complete your Daily Stats Logs and Daily Quest Logs. You will compile these points to earn Treasure Chests in the Treasure Room.

Other Important Terms

Monsters

Monsters are the challenges that come up during Quests that make it challenging to proceed. They often need identification and a battle plan to slay.
- Adventurer's Pro-Tip - Keep track of Monsters you encounter and your battle plans in your Monster guide to refer back to how you have beaten them (and possibly what didn't work) in the past.

Towns & Dungeons

Places you visit on your journey toward completing your Quests. On your Quest World Map you can track your journey by writing in names of towns and dungeons you stop at along the way. Get creative, it's your map. Have fun with it!

QUEST MAPPING

Adventurer,

Before embarking on any journey, it is usually good to have an idea of how you plan to get to your destination. In this case, your destination is the completion of your Quest. Therefore, it is crucial to your success that you create a plan.

When creating quests, remember that there are 4 Basic Elements every quest must have.

- Defined Destination - What do you want to accomplish?
- Trackable Outcome - How will you know the quest is complete? Usually tracked by a number.
- Time Bound - Has an end date, even if it is only an estimate.
- Excitement - This creates a positive future for the adventurer, which they are excited about.

The following parchment will show you the formula for designing extraordinary quests, called Quest Mapping. Quest Mapping ensures you are packed and ready for anything the quest may send your way. It also ensures you don't miss any important steps that will delay your journey.

When monsters show up along the way, be sure to use your monster guide to plan your battle strategy! Keeping a record of what works and what doesn't against each monster will be helpful on future quests and if you come across that monster again on this one!

PRO-Adventurer Tip: While it is important that you map out your journey to the best of your ability, it is also good to remember that most Quests do not go 100% according to plan. So while planning your journey, build in some extra time for detours, monster attacks, and unexpected Sub-Quests.

Happy Questing!

Selina Belle

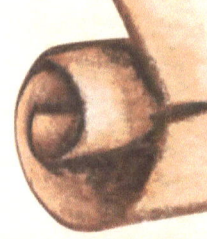

QUEST MAPPING

Write your Main Quest Here!

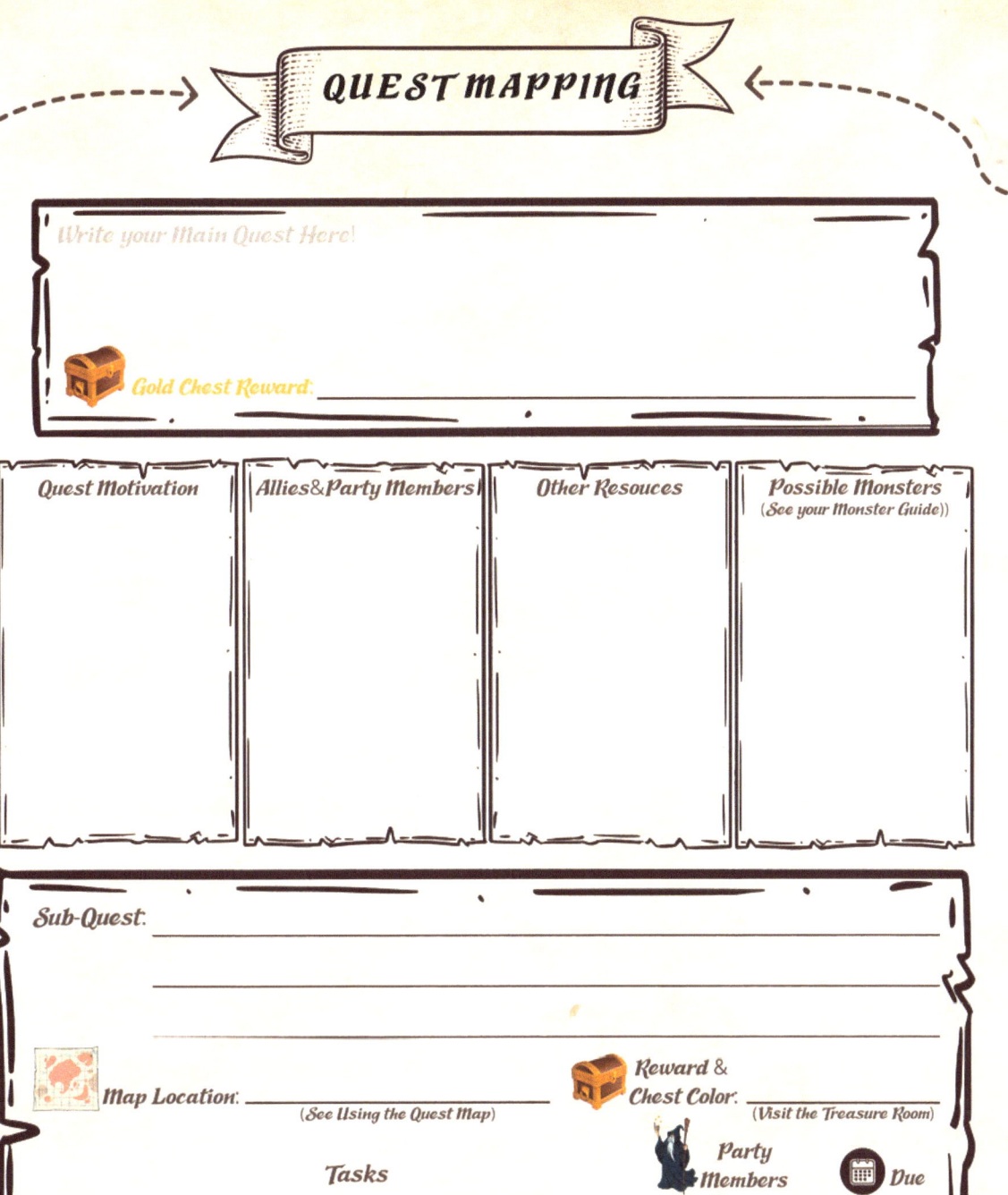

Gold Chest Reward: _____

Quest Motivation	Allies & Party Members	Other Resouces	Possible Monsters (See your Monster Guide))

Sub-Quest: _____

_____

_____

Map Location: _____
(See Using the Quest Map)

Reward & Chest Color: _____
(Visit the Treasure Room)

Tasks **Party Members** **Due**

- ☐ _____
- ☐ _____
- ☐ _____
- ☐ _____
- ☐ _____
- ☐ _____

QUEST MAPPING

Sub-Quest: _____

_____

_____

Map Location: _____

Reward &
Chest Color: _____

Tasks	Party Members	Due
☐ _____	_____	_____
☐ _____	_____	_____
☐ _____	_____	_____
☐ _____	_____	_____
☐ _____	_____	_____
☐ _____	_____	_____

Sub-Quest: _____

_____

_____

Map Location: _____

Reward &
Chest Color: _____

Tasks	Party Members	Due
☐ _____	_____	_____
☐ _____	_____	_____
☐ _____	_____	_____
☐ _____	_____	_____
☐ _____	_____	_____
☐ _____	_____	_____

QUEST MAPPING

Sub-Quest: _____
_____
_____

Map Location: _____

Reward & Chest Color: _____

Tasks

Party Members

📅 Due

- ☐ _____ _____ _____
- ☐ _____ _____ _____
- ☐ _____ _____ _____
- ☐ _____ _____ _____
- ☐ _____ _____ _____
- ☐ _____ _____ _____

Sub-Quest: _____
_____
_____

Map Location: _____

Reward & Chest Color: _____

Tasks

Party Members

📅 Due

- ☐ _____ _____ _____
- ☐ _____ _____ _____
- ☐ _____ _____ _____
- ☐ _____ _____ _____
- ☐ _____ _____ _____
- ☐ _____ _____ _____

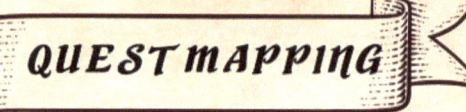

QUEST MAPPING

Sub-Quest: _____
_____
_____

Map Location: _____

Reward &
Chest Color: _____

Tasks

Party Members

Due

- ☐ _____
- ☐ _____
- ☐ _____
- ☐ _____
- ☐ _____
- ☐ _____

Sub-Quest: _____
_____
_____

Map Location: _____

Reward &
Chest Color: _____

Tasks

Party Members

Due

- ☐ _____
- ☐ _____
- ☐ _____
- ☐ _____
- ☐ _____
- ☐ _____

QUEST NOTES

QUEST NOTES

SIDE QUESTS LISTS

Serious
Mapmakers Only!

QUESTING GETS REAL
BEYOND THIS PIOINT

Adventurers
Welcome

Using the Quest Map
Optional Questing Fun for Serious Adventurers

THE WORLD MAP

THE LEGEND

● City

● Village or Town

∩ Dungeon

⌂ Cave

♨ Waypoint or Rest Stop

Adventurer,

When you turn the page of this Tome you will find a beautiful hand-drawn map of the world your Quest may take place in. This map was designed specifically with you, our brave Adventurer, in mind. As you identify parts of your Quest, you may identify locations on the map to travel to in order to carry out that part of your Quest. As you explore this new world, you mark these new locations and name the places you find. (Be creative!)

One day, you may want to revisit this Journal to remember your journey and remind yourself of the amazing adventures you had, new places you traveled to and how you grew as an Adventurer on this Quest.

For printable versions of the map, go to GamifiedLife.net.

Happy Questing!

- Selina Belle

REWARDS & TREASURE

"When questing, it is important to ensure there is a consistent flow of rewards throughout to help keep an adventurer motivated and inspired to continue."
- Selina Belle

Adventurer!

Welcome to the Treasure Room. Um... Just be sure to watch out for dragons.

Throughout the Main Quest, you will receive Treasure Chests as you complete Sub-Quests and daily Treasure Points (TP) as you complete Daily Tasks that accumulate to reach reward levels.

You will select and track your Rewards and Treasure here in the Treasure Room!

Happy Questing!

- Selina Belle

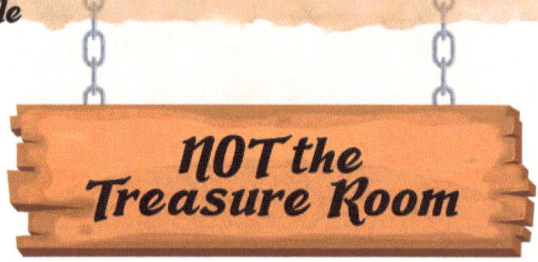

NOT the
Treasure Room

Treasure & Rewards

Brown Treasure Chests - Level 1 rewards.
These rewards are for smaller achievements, like a few days of successful daily journal completion. These rewards should be free or have a low monetary value to them but hold positive value to you. An example may be gifting yourself with a small portion of your favorite snack or 30 minutes to do a fun activity of your choice.

Red Treasure Chest - Level 2 rewards.
These rewards are for smaller but longer term achievements. These rewards should also be free or have a low monetary value to them but hold value to you. An example may be gifting yourself with an hour or two to do a special fun project or an extra hour to play a game. If you choose to spend money on these rewards, they should stay in the range of buying a new book or taking yourself out to dinner.

Blue Treasure Chests - Level 3 rewards.
These rewards are for moderate achievements. These are best for completing a small Sub-Quest or major side quest. If you spend money on these rewards, it should stay in the dining out or going to a movie range. An example may be gifting yourself with a new book and a half-day to relax and read it. Another option may be a nice dinner date with a special someone, or going to a new movie with friends. If plants are your passion, maybe buy a new plant or some flowers for yourself.

Purple Treasure Chests - Level 4 rewards
These rewards are for large achievements on your journey in your Main Quest. Best for the completion of large Sub-Quests. These are a little magical because they propel your journey forward and open up new Sub-Quests for you to embark on! You've put in a lot of energy to complete these Sub-Quests and the rewards should reflect that. These rewards may include taking a day at the beach or hosting a gaming party. Financially, you may choose to invest a little more into this reward. Keep it in line with the Sub-Quest achievement level and what you can afford.

Gold Treasure Chest - Level 5 reward
This is the Top Tier reward! You have completed your Main Quest and have earned a reward suited to the size of the goal! Some Adventurers will take a fun or restful weekend away or host a celebration. Be creative and have fun!

Questing Rewards

Adventurer,

As you complete multi-day Side Quests and Sub-Quests throughout your journey, you will earn Treasure CHESTS! Not to be confused with TP!

These Treasure Chests represent rewards you will identify for yourself before you start any size Quest.

This next part is important!

Identifying your reward before you start the Quest will greatly help you stay motivated on the days you just want to give up or are not in the mood to venture forth.

Below is a guide for assigning treasure chests to your Quests. Once done, go back to your Quest Mapping and assign rewards to your Main Quest and Sub-Quests.

Important Note: Tasks do not get assigned Treasure Chests because completing tasks earn you daily TP when you get to the Daily Quest Logs.

Happy Questing!

 - *Selina Belle*

 Questing Rewards

 Red Chest - Small Side Quests (able to be completed in 2-4 days)

 Blue Chest - Large Side Quests (multiple weeks to complete)
        - Small Sub-Quests (able to be completed in 3 weeks or less, AND does <u>not</u> open new Sub-Quests or have a major impact on the Main Quest.

 Purple Chest - Large Sub-Quests (takes over 3 weeks to complete or opens new Sub-Quests or has a major impact on the Main Quest)

 GOLD Chest - Main Quest Completed! Time to Celebrate!

QUEST REWARD IDEAS

Brown Chest Ideas

Red Chest Ideas

Blue Chest Ideas

Purple Chest Ideas

GOLD Chest Ideas

Treasure Room

Amazing Quests have Amazing Rewards!

When creating amazing Quests, it is important to ensure you have a consistent flow of rewards throughout to help keep an adventurer motivated and inspired to continue. As you are creating your own Quest, you get to choose your rewards!

As you use your Daily Quest Log and Daily Stats Log you earn Treasure Points (TP) by completing certain daily tasks.

As you gather more TP you will earn more Treasure Chests. Each Treasure Chest has a special reward in it!

Your TP accumulates. When you've earned 20 TP, you may receive your reward assigned to that chest.

Write your reward in the space provided. When you have accumulated enough TP, you may open your chest and receive the reward!

Treasure Points	Chest Color	My Reward	Received
20	Brown		☐
40	Brown		☐
60	Brown		☐
80	Brown		☐
100	Red		☐
120	Brown		☐

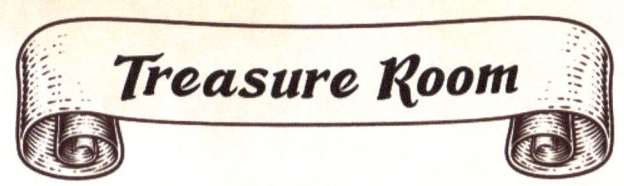

Treasure Room

Treasure Points	Chest Color	My Reward	Received
140	Brown		☐
160	Brown		☐
180	Brown		☐
200	Red		☐
220	Brown		☐
240	Brown		☐
260	Brown		☐
280	Brown		☐
300	Blue		☐
320	Brown		☐
340	Brown		☐
360	Brown		☐

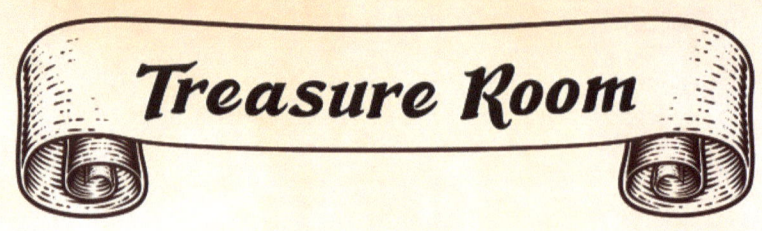

Treasure Room

Treasure Points	Chest Color	My Reward	Received
380	Brown		☐
400	Red		☐
420	Brown		☐
440	Brown		☐
460	Brown		☐
480	Brown		☐
500	Red		☐
520	Brown		☐
540	Brown		☐
560	Brown		☐
580	Brown		☐
600	Purple		☐

Monster Guide

AN ADVENTURER'S STRATEGY GUIDE TO OVERCOMING ANY MONSTER

WRITTEN BY YOU, ADVENTURER

HAPPY QUESTING!

Monster Guide

Adventurer,

Welcome to your Monster Guide! This is where you can log those pesky challenges you encounter on your Quest.

Each challenge you encounter is referred to as a monster, and you get to name each one.

Monster Traits

These are how the monster is showing up for you on the Quest. These are not physical traits of the picture, but rather how you know the monster is there and causing problems. How is it preventing you from moving forward with the Quest? What symptoms are you or your team members experiencing? What have you already tried?

PROSPECT SCARCITY

MONSTER TRAITS

- No new prospects in the customer relationship management (CRM) software.
- Have already contacted everyone I know.
- No engagement on social media posts.

After you have identified all the ways the monster is showing up for you, you can brainstorm strategies to beat it. If you do not have the knowledge or skill set to tackle this monster on your own, this would be a great time to refer back to your Party Members and Allies lists. Once you have mapped out your battle plan, you are ready to take on the Monster and continue on your Quest!

STRATEGIES TO BEAT IT

- Launch online campaign for freebie giveaway leading to upsell
- Join local networking groups (in-person and online)
- Set up 1 to 1 meetings with referral partners to discuss referral opportunities
- Continue brainstorming here!

Monster:

MONSTER TRAITS

_____
_____
_____
_____
_____
_____
_____
_____
_____

_____

STRATEGIES TO BEAT IT

_____
_____
_____
_____
_____
_____
_____
_____
_____
_____
_____
_____
_____
_____
_____
_____
_____
_____
_____

Monster:

MONSTER TRAITS

_____
_____
_____
_____
_____
_____
_____
_____
_____

_____

STRATEGIES TO BEAT IT

_____
_____
_____
_____
_____
_____
_____
_____
_____
_____
_____
_____
_____
_____
_____
_____
_____
_____
_____
_____

Monster:

MONSTER TRAITS

_____
_____
_____
_____
_____
_____
_____
_____
_____
_____

_____

STRATEGIES TO BEAT IT

_____
_____
_____
_____
_____
_____
_____
_____
_____
_____
_____
_____
_____
_____
_____
_____
_____
_____
_____

Monster:

MONSTER TRAITS

_____

STRATEGIES TO BEAT IT

Monster:

_____

MONSTER TRAITS

_____
_____
_____
_____
_____
_____
_____
_____
_____
_____

STRATEGIES TO BEAT IT

_____
_____
_____
_____
_____
_____
_____
_____
_____
_____
_____
_____
_____
_____
_____
_____
_____
_____
_____

Quest Approved!

Adventurer,
Congratulations on designing your quest!
You are ready to begin your journey.
Gather your Allies and Team Members and venture forth.
A new world awaits your discovery!

Happy Questing!
- *Selina Belle*

Let the Quest Begin...

CONGRATULATIONS!
You have earned a Blue Chest for
Completing Questing 101!

Your Logs

 ## How & Why to Use Them

Adventurer,

The weekly planning page, Daily Quest Logs and Daily Stats Logs were designed with the whole adventure in mind. So many times we get caught in the wilderness and become so distracted that we forget to take care of the one resource that matters above all others, ourselves.

It is my hope that through these logs, you remember to plan a successful journey and maintain the self-care necessary to be the best adventurer you can be.

Happy Questing!

- *Selina Belle*

Weekly Planner

The weekly planner was designed so you can take 10 to 15 minutes at the beginning of your week to plan the week's Quest activities, and set a few small wellness goals for yourself that you will need to earn points later in the week!

Bonus! When you complete the weekly planner, you receive an extra 3 TP toward your rewards!

Leisure Planner

It is important that all Adventurers take time to rest and recharge. Some Adventurers prefer to do that alone, while others prefer having friends and family around them. A weekly Leisure Planner is available for you to plan out what activities you will do to recharge each week.

Weekly Check In

Next to the Leisure Planner is a Weekly Check In page for you to tally your weekly TP and review your week.

Special Note About Down Days

Every adventurer deserves a break!

There are going to be days that you are not Questing. Weekends, vacations, sick days, etc. These are considered rest days. Take them and honor them.

This does not mean that you should rest more than you Quest if you are falling behind. However, rest is an important part of recovery, connection with friends and family, and the ability to stay sharp while Questing. No one wants to fall to a monster because they are tired or worn out.

When counting TP, rest days are used in place of completing Quests for those days. You may take 2 TP for Completed Daily Quest as the daily quest is Rest & Leisure! You may also take 3 TP for completing 3 or More Quest Tasks as a gift from us to you for taking a day off.

Weekly Planning Notes

WEEK OF _____

_____

_____

_____

_____

_____

_____

_____

_____

_____

_____

_____

_____

_____

_____

_____

_____

_____

_____

_____

_____

_____

_____

_____

_____

_____

_____

_____

_____

CONGRATULATIONS!
You've earned 3 BONUS TP for completing your Weekly Planner by setting your weekly health goals!

Weekly Planner

WEEK OF _____

MONDAY

TUESDAY

WEDNESDAY

THURSDAY

FRIDAY

SATURDAY

SUNDAY

THIS WEEK'S PRIORITIES

_____
_____
_____

THIS WEEKS HEALTH GOALS:

DRINK ____OZ   ____HOURS

____ BREAKS PER DAY

QUEST & SUB-QUEST NOTES

_____
_____
_____
_____
_____
_____
_____

SIDE QUESTS TO SCHEDULE

_____
_____
_____
_____
_____

MONSTERS TO SLAY

_____
_____
_____
_____
_____
_____

Daily Stats Log

MEALS & MOVEMENT PLANNER

YOUR STATS

WATER INTAKE:

MOVEMENT BREAKS:

SLEEP RATING: 1 2 3 4 5 **HOURS:** _____

NOTES:

MOOD:

HYGIENE:

OTHER:

NOTES, ACHIEVEMENTS & GRATITUDES

_____
_____
_____
_____
_____

REWARD CENTER

When you complete quest and journal items you receive TP. TP is used towards rewards in the Treasure Room!
Be sure to add up your points daily!

Completed Daily Objective (2 TP): ____
Completed 3 or More Quest Tasks (3 TP): ____
Planned & Tracked Meals (1 TP): ____
Drank & Tracked Daily Water Goal (1 TP): ____
Took a minimum of 3 Movement Breaks (1 TP): ____
Completed All 4 Daily Hygiene Activities (1 TP): ____
Wrote at least 2 Achievements & 2 Gratitudes (1 TP): ____

DAILY TOTAL: _____

Daily Quest Log

TODAY'S QUEST

Date:

TODAY'S QUEST TASKS

SIDE QUESTS

ALLIES & PARTY MEMBERS

QUEST JOURNAL

QUEST FINANCIALS

Daily Stats Log

MEALS & MOVEMENT PLANNER

YOUR STATS

WATER INTAKE:

MOVEMENT BREAKS:

SLEEP RATING: **HOURS:**
1 2 3 4 5   _____
NOTES:

MOOD:

HYGIENE:

OTHER:

NOTES , ACHIEVEMENTS & GRATITUDES

_____
_____
_____
_____
_____

 REWARD CENTER

When you complete quest and journal items you receive TP. TP is used towards rewards in the Treasure Room!
Be sure to add up your points daily!

Completed Daily Objective (2 TP): ____
Completed 3 or More Quest Tasks (3 TP): ____
Planned & Tracked Meals (1 TP): ____
Drank & Tracked Daily Water Goal (1 TP): ____
Took a minimum of 3 Movement Breaks (1 TP): ____
Completed All 4 Daily Hygiene Activities (1 TP): ____
Wrote at least 2 Achievements & 2 Gratitudes (1 TP): ____

DAILY TOTAL: _____

Daily Quest Log

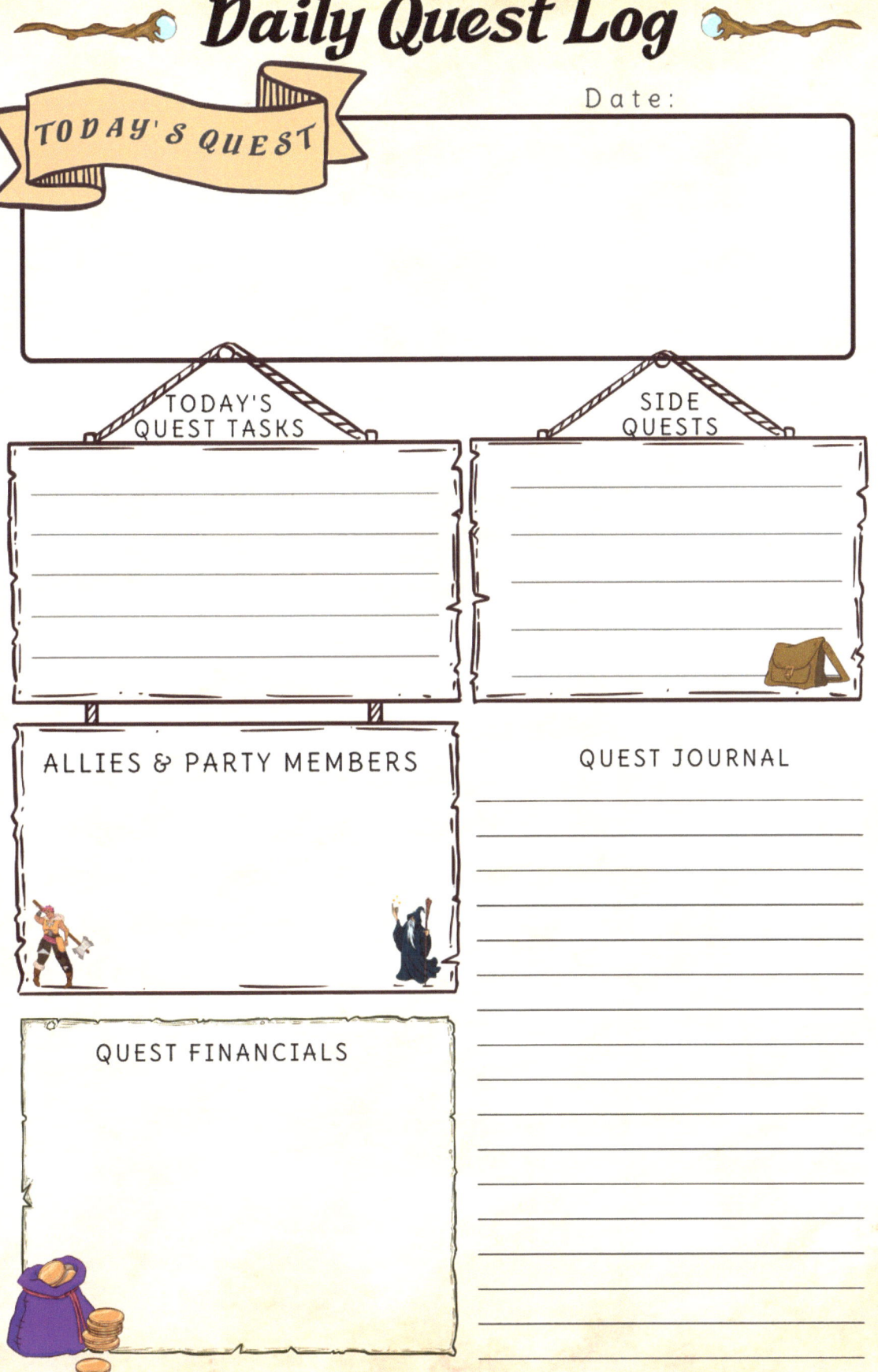

TODAY'S QUEST

Date:

TODAY'S QUEST TASKS

SIDE QUESTS

ALLIES & PARTY MEMBERS

QUEST JOURNAL

QUEST FINANCIALS

Daily Stats Log

MEALS & MOVEMENT PLANNER

YOUR STATS

WATER INTAKE:

MOVEMENT BREAKS:

SLEEP RATING: 1 2 3 4 5 **HOURS:** _____

NOTES:

MOOD:

HYGIENE:

OTHER:

NOTES , ACHIEVEMENTS & GRATITUDES

_____
_____
_____
_____
_____

REWARD CENTER

When you complete quest and journal items you receive TP. TP is used towards rewards in the Treasure Room!
Be sure to add up your points daily!

Completed Daily Objective (2 TP): _____
Completed 3 or More Quest Tasks (3 TP): _____
Planned & Tracked Meals (1 TP): _____
Drank & Tracked Daily Water Goal (1 TP): _____
Took a minimum of 3 Movement Breaks (1 TP): _____
Completed All 4 Daily Hygiene Activities (1 TP): _____
Wrote at least 2 Achievements & 2 Gratitudes (1 TP): _____

DAILY TOTAL: _____

Daily Quest Log

Date:

TODAY'S QUEST TASKS

SIDE QUESTS

ALLIES & PARTY MEMBERS

QUEST JOURNAL

QUEST FINANCIALS

Daily Stats Log

MEALS & MOVEMENT PLANNER

YOUR STATS

WATER INTAKE:

MOVEMENT BREAKS:

SLEEP RATING: **HOURS:**
1 2 3 4 5   _____
NOTES:

MOOD:

HYGIENE:

OTHER:

NOTES , ACHIEVEMENTS & GRATITUDES

_____
_____
_____
_____
_____

 REWARD CENTER

When you complete quest and journal items you receive TP. TP is used towards rewards in the Treasure Room!
Be sure to add up your points daily!

Completed Daily Objective (2 TP): ____
Completed 3 or More Quest Tasks (3 TP): ____
Planned & Tracked Meals (1 TP): ____
Drank & Tracked Daily Water Goal (1 TP): ____
Took a minimum of 3 Movement Breaks (1 TP): ____
Completed All 4 Daily Hygiene Activities (1 TP): ____
Wrote at least 2 Achievements & 2 Gratitudes (1 TP): ____

DAILY TOTAL: _____

Daily Quest Log

TODAY'S QUEST

Date:

TODAY'S QUEST TASKS

SIDE QUESTS

ALLIES & PARTY MEMBERS

QUEST JOURNAL

QUEST FINANCIALS

Daily Stats Log

MEALS & MOVEMENT PLANNER

YOUR STATS

WATER INTAKE:

MOVEMENT BREAKS:

SLEEP RATING: HOURS:
1 2 3 4 5   _____
NOTES:

MOOD:

HYGIENE:

OTHER:

NOTES, ACHIEVEMENTS & GRATITUDES

_____
_____
_____
_____
_____

 REWARD CENTER

When you complete quest and journal items you receive TP. TP is used towards rewards in the Treasure Room!
Be sure to add up your points daily!

Completed Daily Objective (2 TP): ____
Completed 3 or More Quest Tasks (3 TP): ____
Planned & Tracked Meals (1 TP): ____
Drank & Tracked Daily Water Goal (1 TP): ____
Took a minimum of 3 Movement Breaks (1 TP): ____
Completed All 4 Daily Hygiene Activities (1 TP): ____
Wrote at least 2 Achievements & 2 Gratitudes (1 TP): ____

DAILY TOTAL: _____

Daily Quest Log

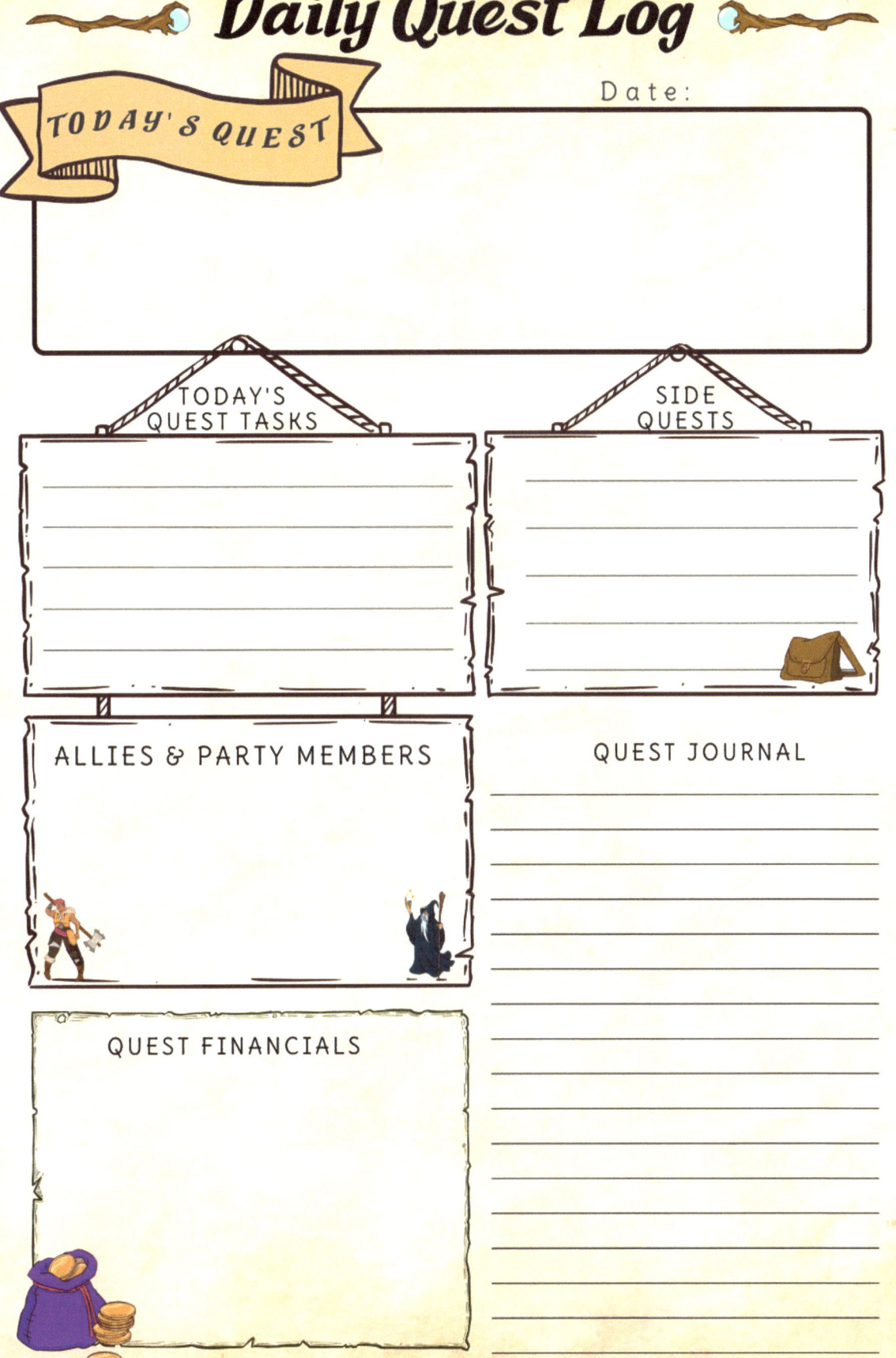

TODAY'S QUEST

Date:

TODAY'S
QUEST TASKS

SIDE
QUESTS

ALLIES & PARTY MEMBERS

QUEST JOURNAL

QUEST FINANCIALS

Daily Stats Log

MEALS & MOVEMENT PLANNER

YOUR STATS

WATER INTAKE:

MOVEMENT BREAKS:

SLEEP RATING: 1 2 3 4 5

HOURS: _____

NOTES:

MOOD:

HYGIENE:

OTHER:

NOTES , ACHIEVEMENTS & GRATITUDES

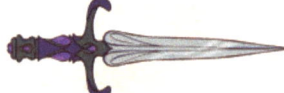

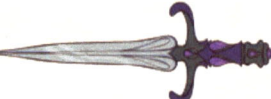

REWARD CENTER

When you complete quest and journal items you receive TP. TP is used towards rewards in the Treasure Room!
Be sure to add up your points daily!

Completed Daily Objective (2 TP): ____
Completed 3 or More Quest Tasks (3 TP): ____
Planned & Tracked Meals (1 TP): ____
Drank & Tracked Daily Water Goal (1 TP): ____
Took a minimum of 3 Movement Breaks (1 TP): ____
Completed All 4 Daily Hygiene Activities (1 TP): ____
Wrote at least 2 Achievements & 2 Gratitudes (1 TP): ____

DAILY TOTAL: _______

Daily Quest Log

TODAY'S QUEST

Date:

TODAY'S QUEST TASKS

SIDE QUESTS

ALLIES & PARTY MEMBERS

QUEST JOURNAL

QUEST FINANCIALS

Daily Stats Log

MEALS & MOVEMENT PLANNER

YOUR STATS

WATER INTAKE:

MOVEMENT BREAKS:

SLEEP RATING: **HOURS:**
1 2 3 4 5   _____

NOTES:

MOOD:

HYGIENE:

OTHER:

NOTES, ACHIEVEMENTS & GRATITUDES

_____

_____

_____

_____

_____

 ## REWARD CENTER

When you complete quest and journal items you receive TP. TP is used towards rewards in the Treasure Room!
Be sure to add up your points daily!

Completed Daily Objective (2 TP): ____
Completed 3 or More Quest Tasks (3 TP): ____
Planned & Tracked Meals (1 TP): ____
Drank & Tracked Daily Water Goal (1 TP): ____
Took a minimum of 3 Movement Breaks (1 TP): ____
Completed All 4 Daily Hygiene Activities (1 TP): ____
Wrote at least 2 Achievements & 2 Gratitudes (1 TP): ____

DAILY TOTAL: _____

Daily Quest Log

TODAY'S QUEST

Date:

TODAY'S QUEST TASKS

SIDE QUESTS

ALLIES & PARTY MEMBERS

QUEST JOURNAL

QUEST FINANCIALS

Leisure Planner

DATE(S) _____

LEISURE ACTIVITES

EVENT DETAILS

LOCATION:

TIME/DURATION:

THEME:

INVITATION LIST

REMIND GUESTS TO BRING

MENU & BEVERAGES

NOTES

Weekly Check In

WEEK OF _____

REWARD CENTER WEEKLY TOTALS

Monday _____
Tuesday _____
Wednesday _____
Thursday _____
Friday _____
Saturday _____
Sunday _____
Bonus 1 _____
Bonus 2 _____

WEEKLY TOTAL: _____

ROLLING TOTAL: _____

PARTY MEMBERS & ALLIES TO THANK THIS WEEK

MONSTERS BEATEN THIS WEEK

NOTES, ACHIEVEMENTS AND GRATITUDES FOR THE WEEK

_____
_____
_____
_____
_____
_____
_____
_____
_____
_____
_____
_____
_____
_____
_____
_____
_____
_____
_____
_____

Journal

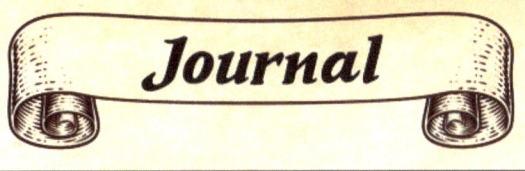

Journal

Journal

Journal

Weekly Planning Notes

WEEK OF _____

_____
_____
_____
_____
_____
_____
_____
_____
_____
_____
_____
_____
_____
_____
_____
_____
_____
_____
_____
_____
_____
_____
_____
_____
_____
_____
_____
_____

CONGRATULATIONS!
You've earned 3 BONUS TP for completing your Weekly planner by setting your weekly health goals!

Weekly Planner

WEEK OF _____

MONDAY

TUESDAY

WEDNESDAY

THURSDAY

FRIDAY

SATURDAY

SUNDAY

THIS WEEK'S PRIORITIES

_____
_____
_____

THIS WEEKS HEALTH GOALS:

DRINK ____ OZ   ____ HOURS

____ BREAKS PER DAY

QUEST & SUB-QUEST NOTES

_____
_____
_____
_____
_____
_____

SIDE QUESTS TO SCHEDULE

_____
_____
_____
_____

MONSTERS TO SLAY

_____
_____
_____
_____
_____
_____

Daily Stats Log

MEALS & MOVEMENT PLANNER

YOUR STATS

WATER INTAKE:

MOVEMENT BREAKS:

SLEEP RATING: HOURS:
1 2 3 4 5   _____

NOTES:

MOOD:

HYGIENE:

OTHER:

NOTES , ACHIEVEMENTS & GRATITUDES

_____
_____
_____
_____
_____

 REWARD CENTER

When you complete quest and journal items you receive TP. TP is used towards rewards in the Treasure Room!
Be sure to add up your points daily!

Completed Daily Objective (2 TP): ____
Completed 3 or More Quest Tasks (3 TP): ____
Planned & Tracked Meals (1 TP): ____
Drank & Tracked Daily Water Goal (1 TP): ____
Took a minimum of 3 Movement Breaks (1 TP): ____
Completed All 4 Daily Hygiene Activities (1 TP): ____
Wrote at least 2 Achievements & 2 Gratitudes (1 TP): ____

DAILY TOTAL: _____

Daily Quest Log

TODAY'S QUEST

Date:

TODAY'S QUEST TASKS

SIDE QUESTS

ALLIES & PARTY MEMBERS

QUEST JOURNAL

QUEST FINANCIALS

Daily Stats Log

MEALS & MOVEMENT PLANNER

YOUR STATS

WATER INTAKE:

MOVEMENT BREAKS:

SLEEP RATING: 1 2 3 4 5   **HOURS:** _____

NOTES:

MOOD:

HYGIENE:

OTHER:

NOTES, ACHIEVEMENTS & GRATITUDES

_____

_____

_____

_____

_____

REWARD CENTER

When you complete quest and journal items you receive TP. TP is used towards rewards in the Treasure Room!
Be sure to add up your points daily!

Completed Daily Objective (2 TP): ____
Completed 3 or More Quest Tasks (3 TP): ____
Planned & Tracked Meals (1 TP): ____
Drank & Tracked Daily Water Goal (1 TP): ____
Took a minimum of 3 Movement Breaks (1 TP): ____
Completed All 4 Daily Hygiene Activities (1 TP): ____
Wrote at least 2 Achievements & 2 Gratitudes (1 TP): ____

DAILY TOTAL: _____

Daily Quest Log

TODAY'S QUEST

Date:

TODAY'S QUEST TASKS

SIDE QUESTS

ALLIES & PARTY MEMBERS

QUEST JOURNAL

QUEST FINANCIALS

Daily Stats Log

MEALS & MOVEMENT PLANNER

YOUR STATS

WATER INTAKE:

MOVEMENT BREAKS:

SLEEP RATING: 1 2 3 4 5 **HOURS:** _____

NOTES:

MOOD:

HYGIENE:

OTHER:

NOTES, ACHIEVEMENTS & GRATITUDES

_____
_____
_____
_____
_____

REWARD CENTER

When you complete quest and journal items you receive TP. TP is used towards rewards in the Treasure Room!
Be sure to add up your points daily!

Completed Daily Objective (2 TP): ____
Completed 3 or More Quest Tasks (3 TP): ____
Planned & Tracked Meals (1 TP): ____
Drank & Tracked Daily Water Goal (1 TP): ____
Took a minimum of 3 Movement Breaks (1 TP): ____
Completed All 4 Daily Hygiene Activities (1 TP): ____
Wrote at least 2 Achievements & 2 Gratitudes (1 TP): ____

DAILY TOTAL: _____

Daily Quest Log

Date:

TODAY'S
QUEST TASKS

SIDE
QUESTS

ALLIES & PARTY MEMBERS

QUEST JOURNAL

QUEST FINANCIALS

Daily Stats Log

MEALS & MOVEMENT PLANNER

YOUR STATS

WATER INTAKE:

MOVEMENT BREAKS:

SLEEP RATING: 1 2 3 4 5 **HOURS:** _____

NOTES:

MOOD:

HYGIENE:

OTHER:

 NOTES , ACHIEVEMENTS & GRATITUDES

_____
_____
_____
_____
_____

 REWARD CENTER

When you complete quest and journal items you receive TP. TP is used towards rewards in the Treasure Room!
Be sure to add up your points daily!

Completed Daily Objective (2 TP): ____
Completed 3 or More Quest Tasks (3 TP): ____
Planned & Tracked Meals (1 TP): ____
Drank & Tracked Daily Water Goal (1 TP): ____
Took a minimum of 3 Movement Breaks (1 TP): ____
Completed All 4 Daily Hygiene Activities (1 TP): ____
Wrote at least 2 Achievements & 2 Gratitudes (1 TP): ____

DAILY TOTAL: _____

Daily Quest Log

TODAY'S QUEST

Date:

TODAY'S QUEST TASKS

SIDE QUESTS

ALLIES & PARTY MEMBERS

QUEST JOURNAL

QUEST FINANCIALS

Daily Stats Log

MEALS & MOVEMENT PLANNER

YOUR STATS

WATER INTAKE:

MOVEMENT BREAKS:

SLEEP RATING: **HOURS:**
1 2 3 4 5 _____
NOTES:

MOOD:

HYGIENE:

OTHER:

NOTES, ACHIEVEMENTS & GRATITUDES

_____
_____
_____
_____
_____

REWARD CENTER

When you complete quest and journal items you receive TP. TP is used towards rewards in the Treasure Room!
Be sure to add up your points daily!

Completed Daily Objective (2 TP): ____
Completed 3 or More Quest Tasks (3 TP): ____
Planned & Tracked Meals (1 TP): ____
Drank & Tracked Daily Water Goal (1 TP): ____
Took a minimum of 3 Movement Breaks (1 TP): ____
Completed All 4 Daily Hygiene Activities (1 TP): ____
Wrote at least 2 Achievements & 2 Gratitudes (1 TP): ____

DAILY TOTAL: _____

Daily Quest Log

Date:

TODAY'S QUEST TASKS

SIDE QUESTS

ALLIES & PARTY MEMBERS

QUEST JOURNAL

QUEST FINANCIALS

Daily Stats Log

MEALS & MOVEMENT PLANNER

YOUR STATS

WATER INTAKE:

MOVEMENT BREAKS:

SLEEP RATING: 1 2 3 4 5 **HOURS:** _____

NOTES:

MOOD:

HYGIENE:

OTHER:

 NOTES , ACHIEVEMENTS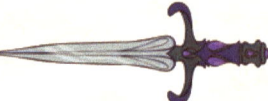
& GRATITUDES

_____
_____
_____
_____
_____

 REWARD CENTER

When you complete quest and journal items you receive TP. TP is used towards rewards in the Treasure Room!
Be sure to add up your points daily!

Completed Daily Objective (2 TP): ____
Completed 3 or More Quest Tasks (3 TP): ____
Planned & Tracked Meals (1 TP): ____
Drank & Tracked Daily Water Goal (1 TP): ____
Took a minimum of 3 Movement Breaks (1 TP): ____
Completed All 4 Daily Hygiene Activities (1 TP): ____
Wrote at least 2 Achievements & 2 Gratitudes (1 TP): ____

DAILY TOTAL: _____

Daily Quest Log

Date:

TODAY'S QUEST TASKS

SIDE QUESTS

ALLIES & PARTY MEMBERS

QUEST JOURNAL

QUEST FINANCIALS

Daily Stats Log

MEALS & MOVEMENT PLANNER

YOUR STATS

WATER INTAKE:

MOVEMENT BREAKS:

SLEEP RATING: 1 2 3 4 5 **HOURS:** _____

NOTES:

MOOD:

HYGIENE:

OTHER:

NOTES , ACHIEVEMENTS & GRATITUDES

_____
_____
_____
_____
_____

REWARD CENTER

When you complete quest and journal items you receive TP. TP is used towards rewards in the Treasure Room!
Be sure to add up your points daily!

Completed Daily Objective (2 TP): ____
Completed 3 or More Quest Tasks (3 TP): ____
Planned & Tracked Meals (1 TP): ____
Drank & Tracked Daily Water Goal (1 TP): ____
Took a minimum of 3 Movement Breaks (1 TP): ____
Completed All 4 Daily Hygiene Activities (1 TP): ____
Wrote at least 2 Achievements & 2 Gratitudes (1 TP): ____

DAILY TOTAL: _____

Daily Quest Log

TODAY'S QUEST

Date:

TODAY'S QUEST TASKS

SIDE QUESTS

ALLIES & PARTY MEMBERS

QUEST JOURNAL

QUEST FINANCIALS

Leisure Planner

DATE(S) _____

LEISURE ACTIVITES

EVENT DETAILS

LOCATION:

TIME/DURATION:

THEME:

INVITATION LIST

REMIND GUESTS TO BRING

MENU & BEVERAGES

NOTES

Weekly Check In

WEEK OF _____

REWARD CENTER WEEKLY TOTALS

Monday _____
Tuesday _____
Wednesday _____
Thursday _____
Friday _____
Saturday _____
Sunday _____
Bonus 1 _____
Bonus 2 _____

WEEKLY TOTAL: _____

ROLLING TOTAL: _____

PARTY MEMBERS & ALLIES TO THANK THIS WEEK

MONSTERS BEATEN THIS WEEK

NOTES, ACHIEVEMENTS AND GRATITUDES FOR THE WEEK

_____
_____
_____
_____
_____
_____
_____
_____
_____
_____
_____
_____
_____
_____
_____
_____
_____
_____
_____
_____
_____

Journal

Journal

Journal

Journal

Weekly Planning Notes

WEEK OF _____

CONGRATULATIONS!
You've earned 3 BONUS TP for completing your Weekly
planner by setting your weekly health goals!

Weekly Planner

MONDAY

TUESDAY

WEDNESDAY

THURSDAY

FRIDAY

SATURDAY

SUNDAY

WEEK OF _____

THIS WEEK'S PRIORITIES

_____
_____

THIS WEEKS HEALTH GOALS:

DRINK ____OZ   ____HOURS

____ BREAKS PER DAY

QUEST & SUB-QUEST NOTES

_____
_____
_____
_____
_____
_____

SIDE QUESTS TO SCHEDULE

_____
_____
_____
_____
_____

MONSTERS TO SLAY

_____
_____
_____
_____
_____

Daily Stats Log

MEALS & MOVEMENT PLANNER

YOUR STATS

WATER INTAKE:

MOVEMENT BREAKS:

SLEEP RATING: 1 2 3 4 5 **HOURS:** _____

NOTES:

MOOD:

HYGIENE:

OTHER:

NOTES , ACHIEVEMENTS & GRATITUDES

_____
_____
_____
_____
_____

 REWARD CENTER

When you complete quest and journal items you receive TP. TP is used towards rewards in the Treasure Room!
Be sure to add up your points daily!

Completed Daily Objective (2 TP): ____
Completed 3 or More Quest Tasks (3 TP): ____
Planned & Tracked Meals (1 TP): ____
Drank & Tracked Daily Water Goal (1 TP): ____
Took a minimum of 3 Movement Breaks (1 TP): ____
Completed All 4 Daily Hygiene Activities (1 TP): ____
Wrote at least 2 Achievements & 2 Gratitudes (1 TP): ____

DAILY TOTAL: _____

Daily Quest Log

TODAY'S QUEST

Date:

TODAY'S QUEST TASKS

SIDE QUESTS

ALLIES & PARTY MEMBERS

QUEST JOURNAL

QUEST FINANCIALS

Daily Stats Log

MEALS & MOVEMENT PLANNER

YOUR STATS

WATER INTAKE:

MOVEMENT BREAKS:

SLEEP RATING: 1 2 3 4 5   **HOURS:** _____

NOTES:

MOOD:

HYGIENE:

OTHER:

NOTES , ACHIEVEMENTS & GRATITUDES

_____

_____

_____

_____

_____

 REWARD CENTER

When you complete quest and journal items you receive TP. TP is used towards rewards in the Treasure Room!
Be sure to add up your points daily!

Completed Daily Objective (2 TP): ____
Completed 3 or More Quest Tasks (3 TP): ____
Planned & Tracked Meals (1 TP): ____
Drank & Tracked Daily Water Goal (1 TP): ____
Took a minimum of 3 Movement Breaks (1 TP): ____
Completed All 4 Daily Hygiene Activities (1 TP): ____
Wrote at least 2 Achievements & 2 Gratitudes (1 TP): ____

DAILY TOTAL: _____

Daily Quest Log

TODAY'S QUEST

Date:

TODAY'S QUEST TASKS

SIDE QUESTS

ALLIES & PARTY MEMBERS

QUEST JOURNAL

QUEST FINANCIALS

Daily Stats Log

MEALS & MOVEMENT PLANNER

YOUR STATS

WATER INTAKE:

MOVEMENT BREAKS:

SLEEP RATING: 1 2 3 4 5 **HOURS:** _____

NOTES:

MOOD:

HYGIENE:

OTHER:

NOTES , ACHIEVEMENTS & GRATITUDES

_____
_____
_____
_____
_____

 REWARD CENTER

When you complete quest and journal items you receive TP. TP is used towards rewards in the Treasure Room!
Be sure to add up your points daily!

Completed Daily Objective (2 TP): ____
Completed 3 or More Quest Tasks (3 TP): ____
Planned & Tracked Meals (1 TP): ____
Drank & Tracked Daily Water Goal (1 TP): ____
Took a minimum of 3 Movement Breaks (1 TP): ____
Completed All 4 Daily Hygiene Activities (1 TP): ____
Wrote at least 2 Achievements & 2 Gratitudes (1 TP): ____

DAILY TOTAL: _____

Daily Quest Log

TODAY'S QUEST

Date:

TODAY'S QUEST TASKS

SIDE QUESTS

ALLIES & PARTY MEMBERS

QUEST JOURNAL

QUEST FINANCIALS

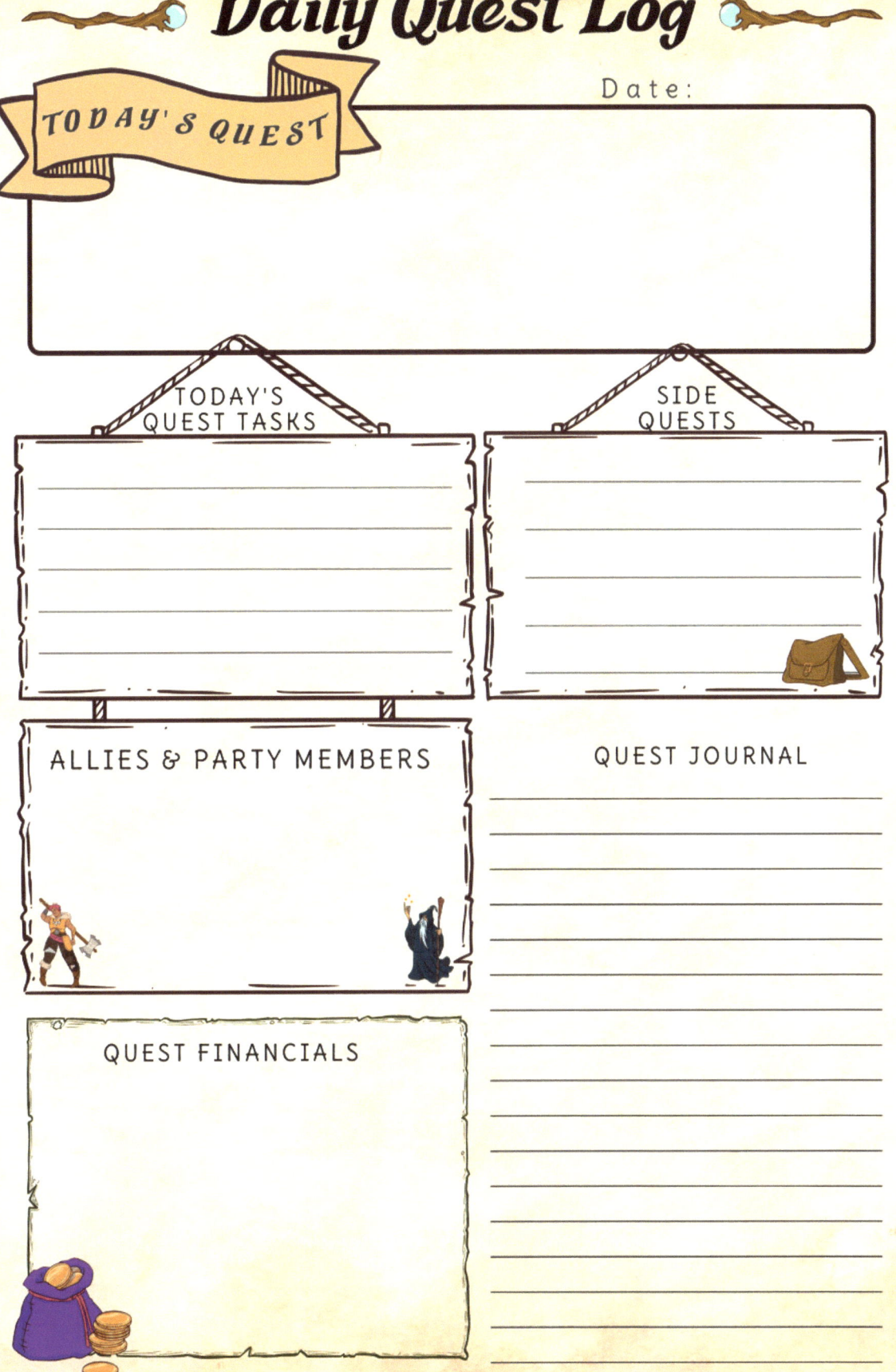

Daily Stats Log

MEALS & MOVEMENT PLANNER

YOUR STATS

WATER INTAKE:

MOVEMENT BREAKS:

SLEEP RATING: HOURS:
1 2 3 4 5   _____

NOTES:

MOOD:

HYGIENE:

OTHER:

NOTES , ACHIEVEMENTS & GRATITUDES

_____
_____
_____
_____
_____

 REWARD CENTER

When you complete quest and journal items you receive TP. TP is used towards rewards in the Treasure Room!
Be sure to add up your points daily!

Completed Daily Objective (2 TP): ____
Completed 3 or More Quest Tasks (3 TP): ____
Planned & Tracked Meals (1 TP): ____
Drank & Tracked Daily Water Goal (1 TP): ____
Took a minimum of 3 Movement Breaks (1 TP): ____
Completed All 4 Daily Hygiene Activities (1 TP): ____
Wrote at least 2 Achievements & 2 Gratitudes (1 TP): ____

DAILY TOTAL: _____

Daily Quest Log

TODAY'S QUEST

Date:

TODAY'S QUEST TASKS

SIDE QUESTS

ALLIES & PARTY MEMBERS

QUEST JOURNAL

QUEST FINANCIALS

Daily Stats Log

YOUR STATS

WATER INTAKE:

MOVEMENT BREAKS:

SLEEP RATING: **HOURS:**

1 2 3 4 5   _____

NOTES:

MOOD:

HYGIENE:

OTHER:

NOTES , ACHIEVEMENTS & GRATITUDES

_____

_____

_____

_____

_____

REWARD CENTER

When you complete quest and journal items you receive TP. TP is used towards rewards in the Treasure Room!
Be sure to add up your points daily!

Completed Daily Objective (2 TP): ____
Completed 3 or More Quest Tasks (3 TP): ____
Planned & Tracked Meals (1 TP): ____
Drank & Tracked Daily Water Goal (1 TP): ____
Took a minimum of 3 Movement Breaks (1 TP): ____
Completed All 4 Daily Hygiene Activities (1 TP): ____
Wrote at least 2 Achievements & 2 Gratitudes (1 TP): ____

DAILY TOTAL: _____

Daily Quest Log

TODAY'S QUEST

Date:

TODAY'S QUEST TASKS

SIDE QUESTS

ALLIES & PARTY MEMBERS

QUEST JOURNAL

QUEST FINANCIALS

Daily Stats Log

MEALS & MOVEMENT PLANNER

YOUR STATS

WATER INTAKE:

MOVEMENT BREAKS:

SLEEP RATING: 1 2 3 4 5

HOURS: _____

NOTES:

MOOD:

HYGIENE:

OTHER:

NOTES , ACHIEVEMENTS & GRATITUDES

____

____

____

____

____

____

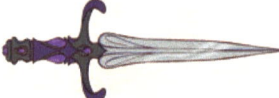

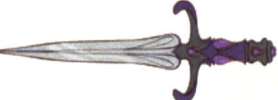

REWARD CENTER

When you complete quest and journal items you receive TP. TP is used towards rewards in the Treasure Room! Be sure to add up your points daily!

Completed Daily Objective (2 TP): ____

Completed 3 or More Quest Tasks (3 TP): ____

Planned & Tracked Meals (1 TP): ____

Drank & Tracked Daily Water Goal (1 TP): ____

Took a minimum of 3 Movement Breaks (1 TP): ____

Completed All 4 Daily Hygiene Activities (1 TP): ____

Wrote at least 2 Achievements & 2 Gratitudes (1 TP): ____

DAILY TOTAL: _______

Daily Quest Log

Date:

TODAY'S QUEST TASKS

SIDE QUESTS

ALLIES & PARTY MEMBERS

QUEST JOURNAL

QUEST FINANCIALS

Daily Stats Log

MEALS & MOVEMENT PLANNER

YOUR STATS

WATER INTAKE:

MOVEMENT BREAKS:

SLEEP RATING: 1 2 3 4 5 **HOURS:** _____

NOTES:

MOOD:

HYGIENE:

OTHER:

NOTES, ACHIEVEMENTS & GRATITUDES

_____
_____
_____
_____
_____

REWARD CENTER

When you complete quest and journal items you receive TP. TP is used towards rewards in the Treasure Room!
Be sure to add up your points daily!

Completed Daily Objective (2 TP): ____
Completed 3 or More Quest Tasks (3 TP): ____
Planned & Tracked Meals (1 TP): ____
Drank & Tracked Daily Water Goal (1 TP): ____
Took a minimum of 3 Movement Breaks (1 TP): ____
Completed All 4 Daily Hygiene Activities (1 TP): ____
Wrote at least 2 Achievements & 2 Gratitudes (1 TP): ____

DAILY TOTAL: _____

Daily Quest Log

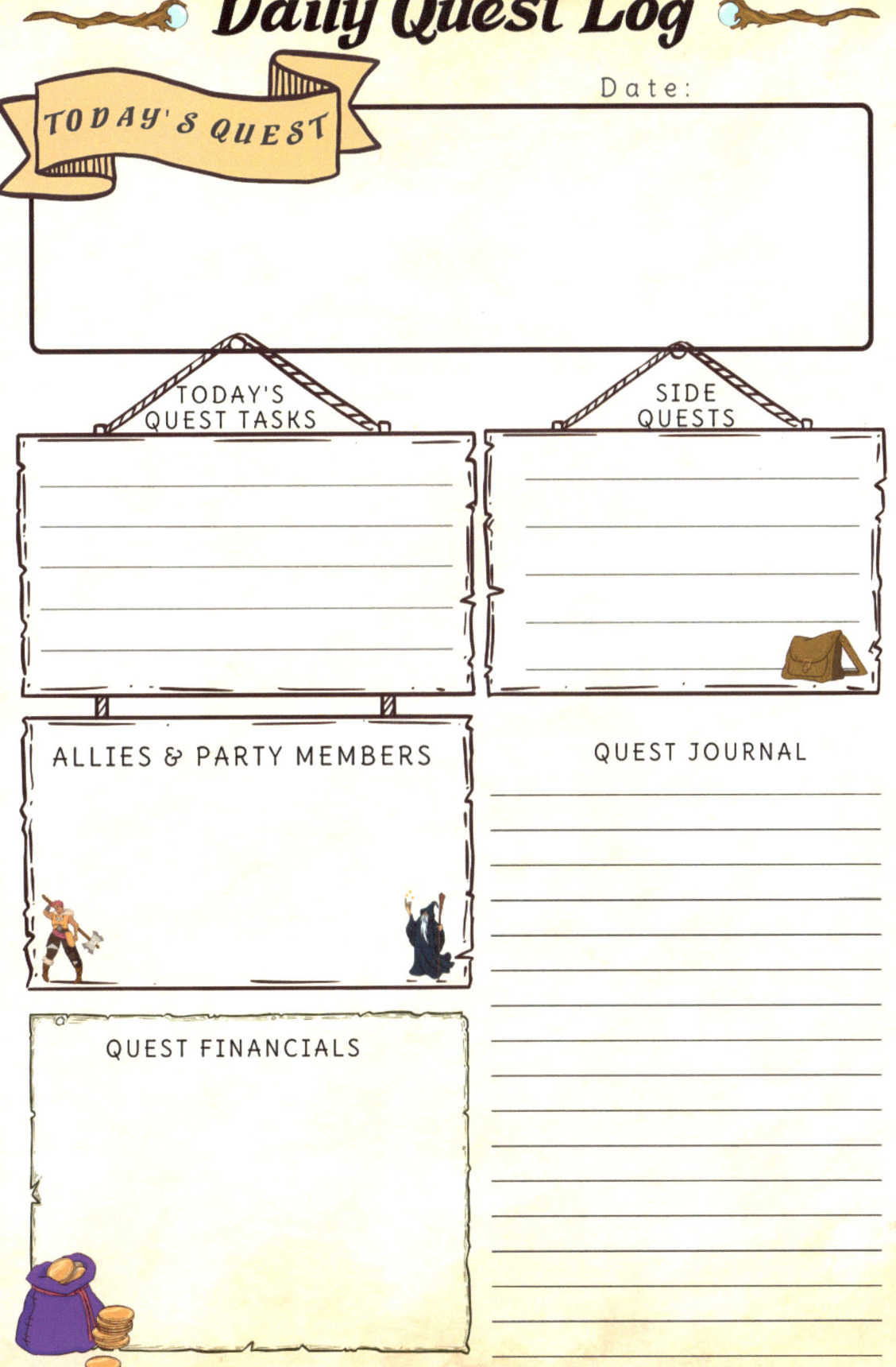

TODAY'S QUEST

Date:

TODAY'S QUEST TASKS

SIDE QUESTS

ALLIES & PARTY MEMBERS

QUEST JOURNAL

QUEST FINANCIALS

Leisure Planner

DATE(S) _____

LEISURE ACTIVITES

EVENT DETAILS

LOCATION:

TIME/DURATION:

THEME:

INVITATION LIST

REMIND GUESTS TO BRING

MENU & BEVERAGES

NOTES

_____
_____
_____
_____
_____
_____
_____
_____

Weekly Check In

WEEK OF _____

REWARD CENTER WEEKLY TOTALS

Monday _____
Tuesday _____
Wednesday _____
Thursday _____
Friday _____
Saturday _____
Sunday _____
Bonus 1 _____
Bonus 2 _____

WEEKLY TOTAL: _____

ROLLING TOTAL: _____

PARTY MEMBERS & ALLIES TO THANK THIS WEEK

MONSTERS BEATEN THIS WEEK

NOTES, ACHIEVEMENTS AND GRATITUDES FOR THE WEEK

Journal

Journal

Journal

Journal

Weekly Planning Notes

WEEK OF _____

CONGRATULATIONS!
You've earned 3 BONUS TP for completing your Weekly
planner by setting your weekly health goals!

Weekly Planner

WEEK OF _____

MONDAY

TUESDAY

WEDNESDAY

THURSDAY

FRIDAY

SATURDAY

SUNDAY

THIS WEEK'S PRIORITIES

_____
_____
_____

THIS WEEKS HEALTH GOALS:

🫗 DRINK ____OZ 💤 ____HOURS

⚔ ____ BREAKS PER DAY

QUEST & SUB-QUEST NOTES

_____
_____
_____
_____
_____
_____
_____

SIDE QUESTS TO SCHEDULE

_____
_____
_____
_____
_____

MONSTERS TO SLAY

_____
_____
_____
_____
_____
_____

Daily Stats Log

MEALS & MOVEMENT PLANNER

YOUR STATS

WATER INTAKE:

MOVEMENT BREAKS:

SLEEP RATING: 1 2 3 4 5 **HOURS:** _____

NOTES:

MOOD:

HYGIENE:

OTHER:

NOTES, ACHIEVEMENTS & GRATITUDES

_____

_____

_____

_____

_____

 REWARD CENTER

When you complete quest and journal items you receive TP. TP is used towards rewards in the Treasure Room!
Be sure to add up your points daily!

Completed Daily Objective (2 TP): ____
Completed 3 or More Quest Tasks (3 TP): ____
Planned & Tracked Meals (1 TP): ____
Drank & Tracked Daily Water Goal (1 TP): ____
Took a minimum of 3 Movement Breaks (1 TP): ____
Completed All 4 Daily Hygiene Activities (1 TP): ____
Wrote at least 2 Achievements & 2 Gratitudes (1 TP): ____

DAILY TOTAL: _____

Daily Quest Log

TODAY'S QUEST

Date:

TODAY'S QUEST TASKS

SIDE QUESTS

ALLIES & PARTY MEMBERS

QUEST JOURNAL

QUEST FINANCIALS

Daily Stats Log

MEALS & MOVEMENT PLANNER

YOUR STATS

WATER INTAKE:

MOVEMENT BREAKS:

SLEEP RATING: 1 2 3 4 5 **HOURS:** _____

NOTES:

MOOD:

HYGIENE:

OTHER:

NOTES, ACHIEVEMENTS & GRATITUDES

_____
_____
_____
_____
_____

REWARD CENTER

When you complete quest and journal items you receive TP. TP is used towards rewards in the Treasure Room!
Be sure to add up your points daily!

Completed Daily Objective (2 TP): ____
Completed 3 or More Quest Tasks (3 TP): ____
Planned & Tracked Meals (1 TP): ____
Drank & Tracked Daily Water Goal (1 TP): ____
Took a minimum of 3 Movement Breaks (1 TP): ____
Completed All 4 Daily Hygiene Activities (1 TP): ____
Wrote at least 2 Achievements & 2 Gratitudes (1 TP): ____

DAILY TOTAL: _____

Daily Quest Log

TODAY'S QUEST

Date:

TODAY'S
QUEST TASKS

SIDE
QUESTS

ALLIES & PARTY MEMBERS

QUEST JOURNAL

QUEST FINANCIALS

Daily Stats Log

MEALS & MOVEMENT PLANNER

YOUR STATS

WATER INTAKE:

MOVEMENT BREAKS:

SLEEP RATING: **HOURS:**
1 2 3 4 5 _____

NOTES:

MOOD:

HYGIENE:

OTHER:

NOTES , ACHIEVEMENTS & GRATITUDES

_____

_____

_____

_____

_____

REWARD CENTER

When you complete quest and journal items you receive TP. TP is used towards rewards in the Treasure Room!
Be sure to add up your points daily!

Completed Daily Objective (2 TP): ____
Completed 3 or More Quest Tasks (3 TP): ____
Planned & Tracked Meals (1 TP): ____
Drank & Tracked Daily Water Goal (1 TP): ____
Took a minimum of 3 Movement Breaks (1 TP): ____
Completed All 4 Daily Hygiene Activities (1 TP): ____
Wrote at least 2 Achievements & 2 Gratitudes (1 TP): ____

DAILY TOTAL: _____

Daily Quest Log

TODAY'S QUEST

Date:

TODAY'S QUEST TASKS

SIDE QUESTS

ALLIES & PARTY MEMBERS

QUEST JOURNAL

QUEST FINANCIALS

Daily Stats Log

MEALS & MOVEMENT PLANNER

YOUR STATS

WATER INTAKE:

MOVEMENT BREAKS:

SLEEP RATING: 1 2 3 4 5   **HOURS:** _____

NOTES:

MOOD:

HYGIENE:

OTHER:

NOTES , ACHIEVEMENTS & GRATITUDES

_____

_____

_____

_____

_____

REWARD CENTER

When you complete quest and journal items you receive TP. TP is used towards rewards in the Treasure Room!
Be sure to add up your points daily!

Completed Daily Objective (2 TP): ____
Completed 3 or More Quest Tasks (3 TP): ____
Planned & Tracked Meals (1 TP): ____
Drank & Tracked Daily Water Goal (1 TP): ____
Took a minimum of 3 Movement Breaks (1 TP): ____
Completed All 4 Daily Hygiene Activities (1 TP): ____
Wrote at least 2 Achievements & 2 Gratitudes (1 TP): ____

DAILY TOTAL: _____

Daily Quest Log

TODAY'S QUEST

Date:

TODAY'S QUEST TASKS

SIDE QUESTS

ALLIES & PARTY MEMBERS

QUEST JOURNAL

QUEST FINANCIALS

Daily Stats Log

MEALS & MOVEMENT PLANNER

YOUR STATS

WATER INTAKE:

MOVEMENT BREAKS:

SLEEP RATING: 1 2 3 4 5   HOURS: _____
NOTES:

MOOD:

HYGIENE:

OTHER:

NOTES, ACHIEVEMENTS & GRATITUDES

_____

_____

_____

_____

_____

 REWARD CENTER

When you complete quest and journal items you receive TP. TP is used towards rewards in the Treasure Room!
Be sure to add up your points daily!

Completed Daily Objective (2 TP): ____
Completed 3 or More Quest Tasks (3 TP): ____
Planned & Tracked Meals (1 TP): ____
Drank & Tracked Daily Water Goal (1 TP): ____
Took a minimum of 3 Movement Breaks (1 TP): ____
Completed All 4 Daily Hygiene Activities (1 TP): ____
Wrote at least 2 Achievements & 2 Gratitudes (1 TP): ____

DAILY TOTAL: _____

Daily Quest Log

TODAY'S QUEST

Date:

TODAY'S QUEST TASKS

SIDE QUESTS

ALLIES & PARTY MEMBERS

QUEST JOURNAL

QUEST FINANCIALS

Daily Stats Log

MEALS & MOVEMENT PLANNER

YOUR STATS

WATER INTAKE:

MOVEMENT BREAKS:

SLEEP RATING: **HOURS:**
1 2 3 4 5   _____

NOTES:

MOOD:

HYGIENE:

OTHER:

NOTES , ACHIEVEMENTS & GRATITUDES

_____

_____

_____

_____

_____

REWARD CENTER

When you complete quest and journal items you receive TP. TP is used towards rewards in the Treasure Room!
Be sure to add up your points daily!

Completed Daily Objective (2 TP): ____
Completed 3 or More Quest Tasks (3 TP): ____
Planned & Tracked Meals (1 TP): ____
Drank & Tracked Daily Water Goal (1 TP): ____
Took a minimum of 3 Movement Breaks (1 TP): ____
Completed All 4 Daily Hygiene Activities (1 TP): ____
Wrote at least 2 Achievements & 2 Gratitudes (1 TP): ____

DAILY TOTAL: _____

Daily Quest Log

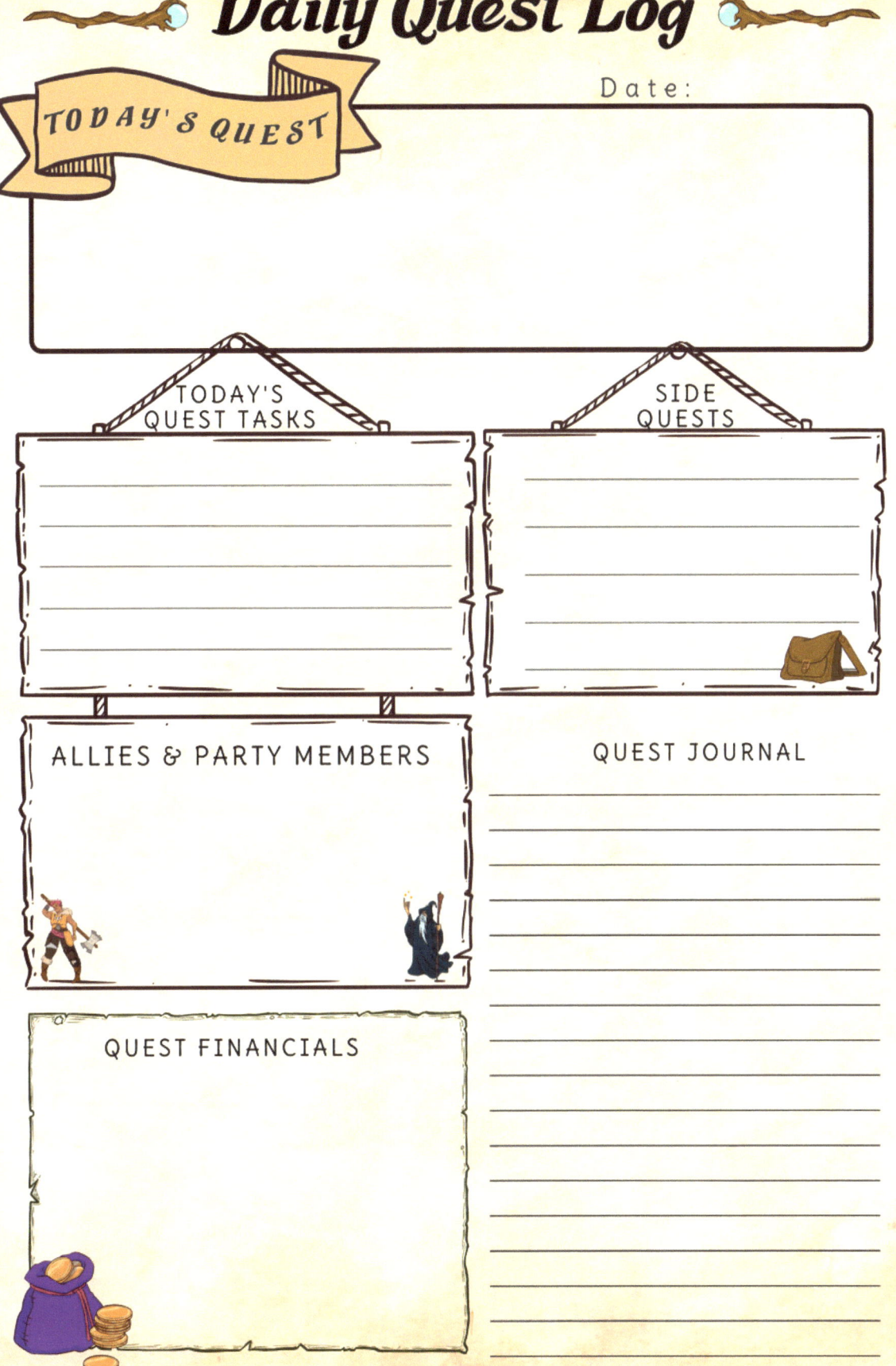

TODAY'S QUEST

Date:

TODAY'S
QUEST TASKS

SIDE
QUESTS

ALLIES & PARTY MEMBERS

QUEST JOURNAL

QUEST FINANCIALS

Daily Stats Log

MEALS & MOVEMENT PLANNER

YOUR STATS

WATER INTAKE:

MOVEMENT BREAKS:

SLEEP RATING: 1 2 3 4 5 **HOURS:** _____

NOTES:

MOOD:

HYGIENE:

OTHER:

NOTES, ACHIEVEMENTS & GRATITUDES

_____
_____
_____
_____
_____

 REWARD CENTER

When you complete quest and journal items you receive TP. TP is used towards rewards in the Treasure Room!
Be sure to add up your points daily!

Completed Daily Objective (2 TP): ____
Completed 3 or More Quest Tasks (3 TP): ____
Planned & Tracked Meals (1 TP): ____
Drank & Tracked Daily Water Goal (1 TP): ____
Took a minimum of 3 Movement Breaks (1 TP): ____
Completed All 4 Daily Hygiene Activities (1 TP): ____
Wrote at least 2 Achievements & 2 Gratitudes (1 TP): ____

DAILY TOTAL: _____

Daily Quest Log

TODAY'S QUEST

Date:

TODAY'S QUEST TASKS

SIDE QUESTS

ALLIES & PARTY MEMBERS

QUEST JOURNAL

QUEST FINANCIALS

Leisure Planner

DATE(S) _____

LEISURE ACTIVITES

EVENT DETAILS

LOCATION:

TIME/DURATION:

THEME:

INVITATION LIST

REMIND GUESTS TO BRING

MENU & BEVERAGES

NOTES

_____
_____
_____
_____
_____
_____
_____

Weekly Check In

WEEK OF _____

REWARD CENTER WEEKLY TOTALS

Monday _____
Tuesday _____
Wednesday _____
Thursday _____
Friday _____
Saturday _____
Sunday _____
Bonus 1 _____
Bonus 2 _____

WEEKLY TOTAL: _____

ROLLING TOTAL: _____

PARTY MEMBERS & ALLIES TO THANK THIS WEEK

MONSTERS BEATEN THIS WEEK

NOTES, ACHIEVEMENTS AND GRATITUDES FOR THE WEEK

Journal

Journal

Journal

Weekly Planning Notes

WEEK OF _____

CONGRATULATIONS!
You've earned 3 BONUS TP for completing your Weekly
planner by setting your weekly health goals!

Weekly Planner

WEEK OF _____

MONDAY

TUESDAY

WEDNESDAY

THURSDAY

FRIDAY

SATURDAY

SUNDAY

THIS WEEK'S PRIORITIES

_____
_____

THIS WEEKS HEALTH GOALS:

DRINK ____ OZ   ____ HOURS

____ BREAKS PER DAY

QUEST & SUB-QUEST NOTES

_____
_____
_____
_____
_____
_____
_____

SIDE QUESTS TO SCHEDULE

_____
_____
_____
_____
_____

MONSTERS TO SLAY

_____
_____
_____
_____
_____
_____
_____

Daily Stats Log

MEALS & MOVEMENT PLANNER

YOUR STATS

WATER INTAKE:

MOVEMENT BREAKS:

SLEEP RATING: 1 2 3 4 5 **HOURS:** _____

NOTES:

MOOD:

HYGIENE:

OTHER:

NOTES, ACHIEVEMENTS & GRATITUDES

_____

_____

_____

_____

_____

 ## REWARD CENTER

When you complete quest and journal items you receive TP. TP is used towards rewards in the Treasure Room!
Be sure to add up your points daily!

Completed Daily Objective (2 TP): ____
Completed 3 or More Quest Tasks (3 TP): ____
Planned & Tracked Meals (1 TP): ____
Drank & Tracked Daily Water Goal (1 TP): ____
Took a minimum of 3 Movement Breaks (1 TP): ____
Completed All 4 Daily Hygiene Activities (1 TP): ____
Wrote at least 2 Achievements & 2 Gratitudes (1 TP): ____

DAILY TOTAL: _____

Daily Quest Log

TODAY'S QUEST

Date:

TODAY'S QUEST TASKS

SIDE QUESTS

ALLIES & PARTY MEMBERS

QUEST JOURNAL

QUEST FINANCIALS

Daily Stats Log

MEALS & MOVEMENT PLANNER

YOUR STATS

WATER INTAKE:

MOVEMENT BREAKS:

SLEEP RATING: **HOURS:**
1 2 3 4 5   _____

NOTES:

MOOD:

HYGIENE:

OTHER:

NOTES, ACHIEVEMENTS & GRATITUDES

_____
_____
_____
_____
_____

REWARD CENTER

When you complete quest and journal items you receive TP. TP is used towards rewards in the Treasure Room!
Be sure to add up your points daily!

Completed Daily Objective (2 TP): ____
Completed 3 or More Quest Tasks (3 TP): ____
Planned & Tracked Meals (1 TP): ____
Drank & Tracked Daily Water Goal (1 TP): ____
Took a minimum of 3 Movement Breaks (1 TP): ____
Completed All 4 Daily Hygiene Activities (1 TP): ____
Wrote at least 2 Achievements & 2 Gratitudes (1 TP): ____

DAILY TOTAL: _____

Daily Quest Log

TODAY'S QUEST

Date:

TODAY'S QUEST TASKS

SIDE QUESTS

ALLIES & PARTY MEMBERS

QUEST JOURNAL

QUEST FINANCIALS

Daily Stats Log

MEALS & MOVEMENT PLANNER

YOUR STATS

WATER INTAKE:

MOVEMENT BREAKS:

SLEEP RATING: 1 2 3 4 5 **HOURS:** _____

NOTES:

MOOD:

HYGIENE:

OTHER:

NOTES, ACHIEVEMENTS & GRATITUDES

_____
_____
_____
_____
_____

 REWARD CENTER

When you complete quest and journal items you receive TP. TP is used towards rewards in the Treasure Room!
Be sure to add up your points daily!

Completed Daily Objective (2 TP): ____
Completed 3 or More Quest Tasks (3 TP): ____
Planned & Tracked Meals (1 TP): ____
Drank & Tracked Daily Water Goal (1 TP): ____
Took a minimum of 3 Movement Breaks (1 TP): ____
Completed All 4 Daily Hygiene Activities (1 TP): ____
Wrote at least 2 Achievements & 2 Gratitudes (1 TP): ____

DAILY TOTAL: _____

Daily Quest Log

TODAY'S QUEST

Date:

TODAY'S QUEST TASKS

SIDE QUESTS

ALLIES & PARTY MEMBERS

QUEST JOURNAL

QUEST FINANCIALS

Daily Stats Log

MEALS & MOVEMENT PLANNER

YOUR STATS

WATER INTAKE:

MOVEMENT BREAKS:

SLEEP RATING: 1 2 3 4 5   **HOURS:** _____

NOTES:

MOOD:

HYGIENE:

OTHER:

NOTES , ACHIEVEMENTS & GRATITUDES

_____

_____

_____

_____

_____

 REWARD CENTER

When you complete quest and journal items you receive TP. TP is used towards rewards in the Treasure Room!
Be sure to add up your points daily!

Completed Daily Objective (2 TP): ____
Completed 3 or More Quest Tasks (3 TP): ____
Planned & Tracked Meals (1 TP): ____
Drank & Tracked Daily Water Goal (1 TP): ____
Took a minimum of 3 Movement Breaks (1 TP): ____
Completed All 4 Daily Hygiene Activities (1 TP): ____
Wrote at least 2 Achievements & 2 Gratitudes (1 TP): ____

DAILY TOTAL: _____

Daily Quest Log

Date:

TODAY'S
QUEST TASKS

SIDE
QUESTS

ALLIES & PARTY MEMBERS

QUEST JOURNAL

QUEST FINANCIALS

Daily Stats Log

MEALS & MOVEMENT PLANNER

YOUR STATS

WATER INTAKE:

MOVEMENT BREAKS:

SLEEP RATING: 1 2 3 4 5 **HOURS:** _____

NOTES:

MOOD:

HYGIENE:

OTHER:

NOTES , ACHIEVEMENTS & GRATITUDES

_____
_____
_____
_____
_____

REWARD CENTER

When you complete quest and journal items you receive TP. TP is used towards rewards in the Treasure Room!
Be sure to add up your points daily!

Completed Daily Objective (2 TP): _____
Completed 3 or More Quest Tasks (3 TP): _____
Planned & Tracked Meals (1 TP): _____
Drank & Tracked Daily Water Goal (1 TP): _____
Took a minimum of 3 Movement Breaks (1 TP): _____
Completed All 4 Daily Hygiene Activities (1 TP): _____
Wrote at least 2 Achievements & 2 Gratitudes (1 TP): _____

DAILY TOTAL: _____

Daily Quest Log

TODAY'S QUEST

Date:

TODAY'S QUEST TASKS

SIDE QUESTS

ALLIES & PARTY MEMBERS

QUEST JOURNAL

QUEST FINANCIALS

Daily Stats Log

MEALS & MOVEMENT PLANNER

YOUR STATS

WATER INTAKE:

MOVEMENT BREAKS:

SLEEP RATING: 1 2 3 4 5 **HOURS:** _____

NOTES:

MOOD:

HYGIENE:

OTHER:

NOTES, ACHIEVEMENTS & GRATITUDES

_____
_____
_____
_____
_____

REWARD CENTER

When you complete quest and journal items you receive TP. TP is used towards rewards in the Treasure Room!
Be sure to add up your points daily!

Completed Daily Objective (2 TP): ____
Completed 3 or More Quest Tasks (3 TP): ____
Planned & Tracked Meals (1 TP): ____
Drank & Tracked Daily Water Goal (1 TP): ____
Took a minimum of 3 Movement Breaks (1 TP): ____
Completed All 4 Daily Hygiene Activities (1 TP): ____
Wrote at least 2 Achievements & 2 Gratitudes (1 TP): ____

DAILY TOTAL: _____

Daily Quest Log

TODAY'S QUEST

Date:

TODAY'S QUEST TASKS

SIDE QUESTS

ALLIES & PARTY MEMBERS

QUEST JOURNAL

QUEST FINANCIALS

Daily Stats Log

MEALS & MOVEMENT PLANNER

YOUR STATS

WATER INTAKE:

MOVEMENT BREAKS:

SLEEP RATING: 1 2 3 4 5 **HOURS:** _____

NOTES:

MOOD:

HYGIENE:

OTHER:

NOTES , ACHIEVEMENTS & GRATITUDES

_____
_____
_____
_____
_____

 REWARD CENTER

When you complete quest and journal items you receive TP. TP is used towards rewards in the Treasure Room!
Be sure to add up your points daily!

Completed Daily Objective (2 TP): ____
Completed 3 or More Quest Tasks (3 TP): ____
Planned & Tracked Meals (1 TP): ____
Drank & Tracked Daily Water Goal (1 TP): ____
Took a minimum of 3 Movement Breaks (1 TP): ____
Completed All 4 Daily Hygiene Activities (1 TP): ____
Wrote at least 2 Achievements & 2 Gratitudes (1 TP): ____

DAILY TOTAL: _____

Daily Quest Log

TODAY'S QUEST

Date:

TODAY'S QUEST TASKS

SIDE QUESTS

ALLIES & PARTY MEMBERS

QUEST JOURNAL

QUEST FINANCIALS

Leisure Planner

DATE(S) _____

LEISURE ACTIVITES

EVENT DETAILS

LOCATION:

TIME/DURATION:

THEME:

INVITATION LIST

REMIND GUESTS TO BRING

MENU & BEVERAGES

NOTES

Weekly Check In

WEEK OF _____

REWARD CENTER WEEKLY TOTALS

Monday _____
Tuesday _____
Wednesday _____
Thursday _____
Friday _____
Saturday _____
Sunday _____
Bonus 1 _____
Bonus 2 _____

WEEKLY TOTAL: _____

ROLLING TOTAL: _____

PARTY MEMBERS & ALLIES TO THANK THIS WEEK

MONSTERS BEATEN THIS WEEK

NOTES, ACHIEVEMENTS AND GRATITUDES FOR THE WEEK

_____
_____
_____
_____
_____
_____
_____
_____
_____
_____
_____
_____
_____
_____
_____
_____
_____
_____

Journal

Journal

Journal

Weekly Planning Notes

WEEK OF _____

CONGRATULATIONS!
You've earned 3 BONUS TP for completing your Weekly
planner by setting your weekly health goals!

Weekly Planner

WEEK OF _____

MONDAY

TUESDAY

WEDNESDAY

THURSDAY

FRIDAY

SATURDAY

SUNDAY

THIS WEEK'S PRIORITIES

_____
_____
_____

THIS WEEKS HEALTH GOALS:

DRINK ____ OZ   ____ HOURS

____ BREAKS PER DAY

QUEST & SUB-QUEST NOTES

_____
_____
_____
_____
_____
_____
_____

SIDE QUESTS TO SCHEDULE

_____
_____
_____
_____
_____
_____

MONSTERS TO SLAY

_____
_____
_____
_____
_____
_____
_____

Daily Stats Log

MEALS & MOVEMENT PLANNER

YOUR STATS

WATER INTAKE:

MOVEMENT BREAKS:

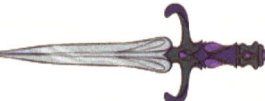

SLEEP RATING: 1 2 3 4 5   **HOURS:** _____

NOTES:

MOOD:

HYGIENE:

OTHER:

NOTES, ACHIEVEMENTS & GRATITUDES

_____
_____
_____
_____
_____

REWARD CENTER

When you complete quest and journal items you receive TP. TP is used towards rewards in the Treasure Room!
Be sure to add up your points daily!

Completed Daily Objective (2 TP): ____
Completed 3 or More Quest Tasks (3 TP): ____
Planned & Tracked Meals (1 TP): ____
Drank & Tracked Daily Water Goal (1 TP): ____
Took a minimum of 3 Movement Breaks (1 TP): ____
Completed All 4 Daily Hygiene Activities (1 TP): ____
Wrote at least 2 Achievements & 2 Gratitudes (1 TP): ____

DAILY TOTAL: _____

Daily Quest Log

TODAY'S QUEST

Date:

TODAY'S QUEST TASKS

SIDE QUESTS

ALLIES & PARTY MEMBERS

QUEST JOURNAL

QUEST FINANCIALS

Daily Stats Log

MEALS & MOVEMENT PLANNER

YOUR STATS

WATER INTAKE:

MOVEMENT BREAKS:

SLEEP RATING: 1 2 3 4 5 **HOURS:** _____

NOTES:

MOOD:

HYGIENE:

OTHER:

NOTES , ACHIEVEMENTS & GRATITUDES

_____

_____

_____

_____

_____

 ### REWARD CENTER

When you complete quest and journal items you receive TP. TP is used towards rewards in the Treasure Room!
Be sure to add up your points daily!

Completed Daily Objective (2 TP): ____
Completed 3 or More Quest Tasks (3 TP): ____
Planned & Tracked Meals (1 TP): ____
Drank & Tracked Daily Water Goal (1 TP): ____
Took a minimum of 3 Movement Breaks (1 TP): ____
Completed All 4 Daily Hygiene Activities (1 TP): ____
Wrote at least 2 Achievements & 2 Gratitudes (1 TP): ____

DAILY TOTAL: _____

Daily Quest Log

TODAY'S QUEST

Date:

TODAY'S QUEST TASKS

SIDE QUESTS

ALLIES & PARTY MEMBERS

QUEST JOURNAL

QUEST FINANCIALS

Daily Stats Log

MEALS & MOVEMENT PLANNER

YOUR STATS

WATER INTAKE:

MOVEMENT BREAKS:

SLEEP RATING: HOURS:
1 2 3 4 5   _____

NOTES:

MOOD:

HYGIENE:

OTHER:

 NOTES , ACHIEVEMENTS
& GRATITUDES

_____

_____

_____

_____

_____

 ## REWARD CENTER

When you complete quest and
journal items you receive TP.
TP is used towards rewards in
the Treasure Room!
Be sure to add up your points
daily!

Completed Daily Objective (2 TP): ____
Completed 3 or More Quest Tasks (3 TP): ____
Planned & Tracked Meals (1 TP): ____
Drank & Tracked Daily Water Goal (1 TP): ____
Took a minimum of 3 Movement Breaks (1 TP): ____
Completed All 4 Daily Hygiene Activities (1 TP): ____
Wrote at least 2 Achievements & 2 Gratitudes (1 TP): ____

DAILY TOTAL: _____

Daily Quest Log

TODAY'S QUEST

Date:

TODAY'S QUEST TASKS

SIDE QUESTS

ALLIES & PARTY MEMBERS

QUEST JOURNAL

QUEST FINANCIALS

Daily Stats Log

MEALS & MOVEMENT PLANNER

YOUR STATS

WATER INTAKE:

MOVEMENT BREAKS:

SLEEP RATING: HOURS:
1 2 3 4 5   _____

NOTES:

MOOD:

HYGIENE:

OTHER:

NOTES , ACHIEVEMENTS & GRATITUDES

_____
_____
_____
_____
_____

REWARD CENTER

When you complete quest and journal items you receive TP. TP is used towards rewards in the Treasure Room!
Be sure to add up your points daily!

Completed Daily Objective (2 TP): ____
Completed 3 or More Quest Tasks (3 TP): ____
Planned & Tracked Meals (1 TP): ____
Drank & Tracked Daily Water Goal (1 TP): ____
Took a minimum of 3 Movement Breaks (1 TP): ____
Completed All 4 Daily Hygiene Activities (1 TP): ____
Wrote at least 2 Achievements & 2 Gratitudes (1 TP): ____

DAILY TOTAL: _____

Daily Quest Log

TODAY'S QUEST

Date:

TODAY'S QUEST TASKS

SIDE QUESTS

ALLIES & PARTY MEMBERS

QUEST JOURNAL

QUEST FINANCIALS

Daily Stats Log

MEALS & MOVEMENT PLANNER

YOUR STATS

WATER INTAKE:

MOVEMENT BREAKS:

SLEEP RATING: 1 2 3 4 5 **HOURS:** _____

NOTES:

MOOD:

HYGIENE:

OTHER:

NOTES, ACHIEVEMENTS & GRATITUDES

_____

_____

_____

_____

_____

 ## REWARD CENTER

When you complete quest and journal items you receive TP. TP is used towards rewards in the Treasure Room!
Be sure to add up your points daily!

Completed Daily Objective (2 TP): ____
Completed 3 or More Quest Tasks (3 TP): ____
Planned & Tracked Meals (1 TP): ____
Drank & Tracked Daily Water Goal (1 TP): ____
Took a minimum of 3 Movement Breaks (1 TP): ____
Completed All 4 Daily Hygiene Activities (1 TP): ____
Wrote at least 2 Achievements & 2 Gratitudes (1 TP): ____

DAILY TOTAL: _____

Daily Quest Log

TODAY'S QUEST

Date:

TODAY'S QUEST TASKS

SIDE QUESTS

ALLIES & PARTY MEMBERS

QUEST JOURNAL

QUEST FINANCIALS

Daily Stats Log

MEALS & MOVEMENT PLANNER

YOUR STATS

WATER INTAKE:

MOVEMENT BREAKS:

SLEEP RATING: **HOURS:**
Zzz...   1 2 3 4 5   _ _ _ _ _
NOTES:

MOOD:

HYGIENE:

OTHER:

NOTES , ACHIEVEMENTS & GRATITUDES

_____
_____
_____
_____
_____

REWARD CENTER

When you complete quest and journal items you receive TP. TP is used towards rewards in the Treasure Room!
Be sure to add up your points daily!

Completed Daily Objective (2 TP): ____
Completed 3 or More Quest Tasks (3 TP): ____
Planned & Tracked Meals (1 TP): ____
Drank & Tracked Daily Water Goal (1 TP): ____
Took a minimum of 3 Movement Breaks (1 TP): ____
Completed All 4 Daily Hygiene Activities (1 TP): ____
Wrote at least 2 Achievements & 2 Gratitudes (1 TP): ____

DAILY TOTAL: _____

Daily Quest Log

TODAY'S QUEST

Date:

TODAY'S QUEST TASKS

SIDE QUESTS

ALLIES & PARTY MEMBERS

QUEST JOURNAL

QUEST FINANCIALS

Daily Stats Log

MEALS & MOVEMENT PLANNER

YOUR STATS

WATER INTAKE:

MOVEMENT BREAKS:

SLEEP RATING: HOURS:
1 2 3 4 5   _____
NOTES:

MOOD:

HYGIENE:

OTHER:

NOTES, ACHIEVEMENTS & GRATITUDES

_____
_____
_____
_____
_____

 ## REWARD CENTER

When you complete quest and journal items you receive TP. TP is used towards rewards in the Treasure Room!
Be sure to add up your points daily!

Completed Daily Objective (2 TP): ____
Completed 3 or More Quest Tasks (3 TP): ____
Planned & Tracked Meals (1 TP): ____
Drank & Tracked Daily Water Goal (1 TP): ____
Took a minimum of 3 Movement Breaks (1 TP): ____
Completed All 4 Daily Hygiene Activities (1 TP): ____
Wrote at least 2 Achievements & 2 Gratitudes (1 TP): ____

DAILY TOTAL: _____

Daily Quest Log

TODAY'S QUEST

Date:

TODAY'S QUEST TASKS

SIDE QUESTS

ALLIES & PARTY MEMBERS

QUEST JOURNAL

QUEST FINANCIALS

Leisure Planner

DATE(S) _____

LEISURE ACTIVITES

EVENT DETAILS

LOCATION:

TIME/DURATION:

THEME:

INVITATION LIST

REMIND GUESTS TO BRING

MENU & BEVERAGES

NOTES

_____
_____
_____
_____
_____
_____
_____
_____

Weekly Check In

WEEK OF _____

REWARD CENTER WEEKLY TOTALS

Monday _____
Tuesday _____
Wednesday _____
Thursday _____
Friday _____
Saturday _____
Sunday _____
Bonus 1 _____
Bonus 2 _____

WEEKLY TOTAL: _____

ROLLING TOTAL: _____

PARTY MEMBERS & ALLIES TO THANK THIS WEEK

MONSTERS BEATEN THIS WEEK

NOTES, ACHIEVEMENTS AND GRATITUDES FOR THE WEEK

Journal

Journal

Journal

Weekly Planning Notes

WEEK OF _____

_____
_____
_____
_____
_____
_____
_____
_____
_____
_____
_____
_____
_____
_____
_____
_____
_____
_____
_____
_____
_____
_____
_____
_____
_____
_____

CONGRATULATIONS!
You've earned 3 BONUS TP for completing your Weekly
planner by setting your weekly health goals!

Weekly Planner

MONDAY

TUESDAY

WEDNESDAY

THURSDAY

FRIDAY

SATURDAY

SUNDAY

WEEK OF _____

THIS WEEK'S PRIORITIES

_____
_____
_____

THIS WEEKS HEALTH GOALS:

DRINK ____ OZ   ____ HOURS

____ BREAKS PER DAY

QUEST & SUB-QUEST NOTES

_____
_____
_____
_____
_____
_____
_____
_____

SIDE QUESTS TO SCHEDULE

_____
_____
_____
_____
_____
_____

MONSTERS TO SLAY

_____
_____
_____
_____
_____
_____
_____

Daily Stats Log

MEALS & MOVEMENT PLANNER

YOUR STATS

WATER INTAKE:

MOVEMENT BREAKS:

SLEEP RATING: 1 2 3 4 5 **HOURS:** _____

NOTES:

MOOD:

HYGIENE:

OTHER:

NOTES, ACHIEVEMENTS & GRATITUDES

_____

_____

_____

_____

_____

 REWARD CENTER

When you complete quest and journal items you receive TP. TP is used towards rewards in the Treasure Room!
Be sure to add up your points daily!

Completed Daily Objective (2 TP): ____
Completed 3 or More Quest Tasks (3 TP): ____
Planned & Tracked Meals (1 TP): ____
Drank & Tracked Daily Water Goal (1 TP): ____
Took a minimum of 3 Movement Breaks (1 TP): ____
Completed All 4 Daily Hygiene Activities (1 TP): ____
Wrote at least 2 Achievements & 2 Gratitudes (1 TP): ____

DAILY TOTAL: _____

Daily Quest Log

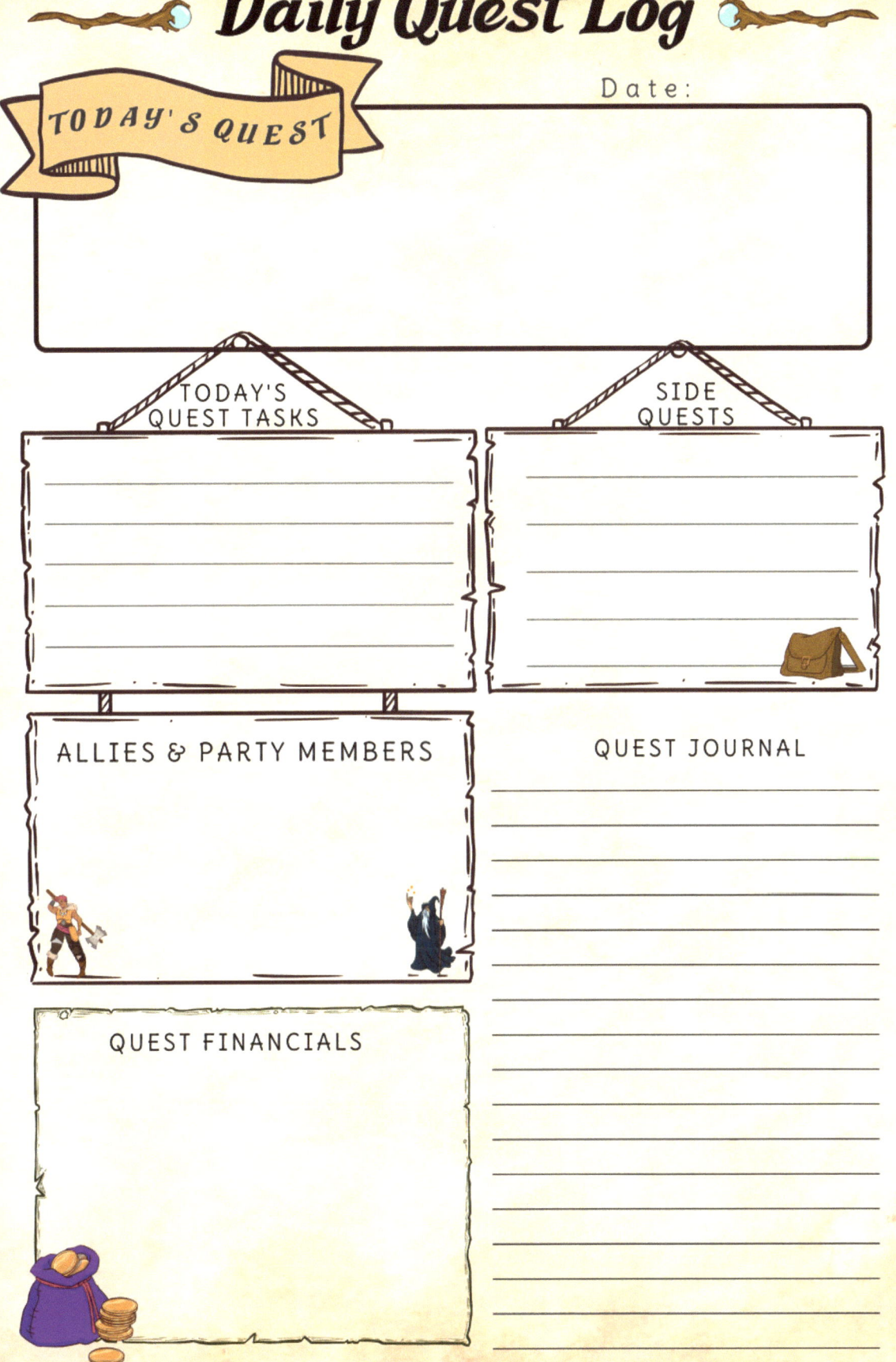

TODAY'S QUEST

Date:

TODAY'S QUEST TASKS

SIDE QUESTS

ALLIES & PARTY MEMBERS

QUEST JOURNAL

QUEST FINANCIALS

Daily Stats Log

MEALS & MOVEMENT PLANNER

YOUR STATS

WATER INTAKE:

MOVEMENT BREAKS:

SLEEP RATING: **HOURS:**
Zzz... 1 2 3 4 5   _____

NOTES:

MOOD:

HYGIENE:

OTHER:

 NOTES , ACHIEVEMENTS & GRATITUDES

_____
_____
_____
_____
_____

REWARD CENTER

When you complete quest and journal items you receive TP. TP is used towards rewards in the Treasure Room!
Be sure to add up your points daily!

Completed Daily Objective (2 TP): ____
Completed 3 or More Quest Tasks (3 TP): ____
Planned & Tracked Meals (1 TP): ____
Drank & Tracked Daily Water Goal (1 TP): ____
Took a minimum of 3 Movement Breaks (1 TP): ____
Completed All 4 Daily Hygiene Activities (1 TP): ____
Wrote at least 2 Achievements & 2 Gratitudes (1 TP): ____

DAILY TOTAL: _____

Daily Quest Log

TODAY'S QUEST

Date:

TODAY'S QUEST TASKS

SIDE QUESTS

ALLIES & PARTY MEMBERS

QUEST JOURNAL

QUEST FINANCIALS

Daily Stats Log

MEALS & MOVEMENT PLANNER

YOUR STATS

WATER INTAKE:

MOVEMENT BREAKS:

SLEEP RATING: 1 2 3 4 5   **HOURS:** _____

NOTES:

MOOD:

HYGIENE:

OTHER:

NOTES , ACHIEVEMENTS & GRATITUDES

_____
_____
_____
_____
_____

REWARD CENTER

When you complete quest and journal items you receive TP. TP is used towards rewards in the Treasure Room!
Be sure to add up your points daily!

Completed Daily Objective (2 TP): ____
Completed 3 or More Quest Tasks (3 TP): ____
Planned & Tracked Meals (1 TP): ____
Drank & Tracked Daily Water Goal (1 TP): ____
Took a minimum of 3 Movement Breaks (1 TP): ____
Completed All 4 Daily Hygiene Activities (1 TP): ____
Wrote at least 2 Achievements & 2 Gratitudes (1 TP): ____

DAILY TOTAL: _____

Daily Quest Log

TODAY'S QUEST

Date:

TODAY'S QUEST TASKS

SIDE QUESTS

ALLIES & PARTY MEMBERS

QUEST JOURNAL

QUEST FINANCIALS

Daily Stats Log

MEALS & MOVEMENT PLANNER

YOUR STATS

WATER INTAKE:

MOVEMENT BREAKS:

SLEEP RATING: 1 2 3 4 5 **HOURS:** _____

NOTES:

MOOD:

HYGIENE:

OTHER:

NOTES, ACHIEVEMENTS & GRATITUDES

_____

_____

_____

_____

_____

REWARD CENTER

When you complete quest and journal items you receive TP. TP is used towards rewards in the Treasure Room!
Be sure to add up your points daily!

Completed Daily Objective (2 TP): _____
Completed 3 or More Quest Tasks (3 TP): _____
Planned & Tracked Meals (1 TP): _____
Drank & Tracked Daily Water Goal (1 TP): _____
Took a minimum of 3 Movement Breaks (1 TP): _____
Completed All 4 Daily Hygiene Activities (1 TP): _____
Wrote at least 2 Achievements & 2 Gratitudes (1 TP): _____

DAILY TOTAL: _____

Daily Quest Log

Date:

TODAY'S QUEST

TODAY'S QUEST TASKS

SIDE QUESTS

ALLIES & PARTY MEMBERS

QUEST JOURNAL

QUEST FINANCIALS

Daily Stats Log

YOUR STATS

WATER INTAKE:

MOVEMENT BREAKS:

SLEEP RATING: 1 2 3 4 5 **HOURS:** _____

NOTES:

MOOD:

HYGIENE:

OTHER:

NOTES, ACHIEVEMENTS & GRATITUDES

_____
_____
_____
_____
_____

REWARD CENTER

When you complete quest and journal items you receive TP. TP is used towards rewards in the Treasure Room!
Be sure to add up your points daily!

Completed Daily Objective (2 TP): ____
Completed 3 or More Quest Tasks (3 TP): ____
Planned & Tracked Meals (1 TP): ____
Drank & Tracked Daily Water Goal (1 TP): ____
Took a minimum of 3 Movement Breaks (1 TP): ____
Completed All 4 Daily Hygiene Activities (1 TP): ____
Wrote at least 2 Achievements & 2 Gratitudes (1 TP): ____

DAILY TOTAL: _____

Daily Quest Log

Date:

TODAY'S QUEST TASKS

SIDE QUESTS

ALLIES & PARTY MEMBERS

QUEST JOURNAL

QUEST FINANCIALS

Daily Stats Log

MEALS & MOVEMENT PLANNER

YOUR STATS

WATER INTAKE:

MOVEMENT BREAKS:

SLEEP RATING: **HOURS:**
1 2 3 4 5   _____
NOTES:

MOOD:

HYGIENE:

OTHER:

NOTES, ACHIEVEMENTS & GRATITUDES

_____
_____
_____
_____
_____

 REWARD CENTER

When you complete quest and journal items you receive TP. TP is used towards rewards in the Treasure Room!
Be sure to add up your points daily!

Completed Daily Objective (2 TP): ____
Completed 3 or More Quest Tasks (3 TP): ____
Planned & Tracked Meals (1 TP): ____
Drank & Tracked Daily Water Goal (1 TP): ____
Took a minimum of 3 Movement Breaks (1 TP): ____
Completed All 4 Daily Hygiene Activities (1 TP): ____
Wrote at least 2 Achievements & 2 Gratitudes (1 TP): ____

DAILY TOTAL: _____

Daily Quest Log

TODAY'S QUEST

Date:

TODAY'S QUEST TASKS

SIDE QUESTS

ALLIES & PARTY MEMBERS

QUEST JOURNAL

QUEST FINANCIALS

Daily Stats Log

MEALS & MOVEMENT PLANNER

YOUR STATS

WATER INTAKE:

MOVEMENT BREAKS:

SLEEP RATING: 1 2 3 4 5 **HOURS:** _____

NOTES:

MOOD:

HYGIENE:

OTHER:

 NOTES , ACHIEVEMENTS & GRATITUDES

_____

_____

_____

_____

_____

 REWARD CENTER

When you complete quest and journal items you receive TP. TP is used towards rewards in the Treasure Room!
Be sure to add up your points daily!

Completed Daily Objective (2 TP): ____

Completed 3 or More Quest Tasks (3 TP): ____

Planned & Tracked Meals (1 TP): ____

Drank & Tracked Daily Water Goal (1 TP): ____

Took a minimum of 3 Movement Breaks (1 TP): ____

Completed All 4 Daily Hygiene Activities (1 TP): ____

Wrote at least 2 Achievements & 2 Gratitudes (1 TP): ____

DAILY TOTAL: _____

Daily Quest Log

TODAY'S QUEST

Date:

TODAY'S QUEST TASKS

SIDE QUESTS

ALLIES & PARTY MEMBERS

QUEST JOURNAL

QUEST FINANCIALS

Leisure Planner

DATE(S) _____

LEISURE ACTIVITES

EVENT DETAILS

LOCATION:

TIME/DURATION:

THEME:

INVITATION LIST

REMIND GUESTS TO BRING

MENU & BEVERAGES

NOTES

_____
_____
_____
_____
_____
_____
_____

Weekly Check In

WEEK OF _____

REWARD CENTER WEEKLY TOTALS

Monday _____
Tuesday _____
Wednesday _____
Thursday _____
Friday _____
Saturday _____
Sunday _____
Bonus 1 _____
Bonus 2 _____

WEEKLY TOTAL: _____

ROLLING TOTAL: _____

PARTY MEMBERS & ALLIES TO THANK THIS WEEK

MONSTERS BEATEN THIS WEEK

NOTES, ACHIEVEMENTS AND GRATITUDES FOR THE WEEK

_____
_____
_____
_____
_____
_____
_____
_____
_____
_____
_____
_____
_____
_____
_____
_____
_____
_____
_____
_____
_____

Journal

Journal

Journal

Weekly Planning Notes

WEEK OF _____

_____
_____
_____
_____
_____
_____
_____
_____
_____
_____
_____
_____
_____
_____
_____
_____
_____
_____
_____
_____
_____
_____
_____
_____
_____

CONGRATULATIONS!
You've earned 3 BONUS TP for completing your Weekly
planner by setting your weekly health goals!

Weekly Planner

WEEK OF _____

MONDAY

TUESDAY

WEDNESDAY

THURSDAY

FRIDAY

SATURDAY

SUNDAY

THIS WEEK'S PRIORITIES

_____
_____
_____

THIS WEEKS HEALTH GOALS:

DRINK ____OZ   ____HOURS

____ BREAKS PER DAY

QUEST & SUB-QUEST NOTES

_____
_____
_____
_____
_____
_____
_____

SIDE QUESTS TO SCHEDULE

_____
_____
_____
_____

MONSTERS TO SLAY

_____
_____
_____
_____
_____

Daily Stats Log

MEALS & MOVEMENT PLANNER

YOUR STATS

WATER INTAKE:

MOVEMENT BREAKS:

SLEEP RATING: HOURS:
1 2 3 4 5   _____

NOTES:

MOOD:

HYGIENE:

OTHER:

NOTES , ACHIEVEMENTS & GRATITUDES

_____

_____

_____

_____

_____

 REWARD CENTER

When you complete quest and journal items you receive TP. TP is used towards rewards in the Treasure Room!
Be sure to add up your points daily!

Completed Daily Objective (2 TP): ____
Completed 3 or More Quest Tasks (3 TP): ____
Planned & Tracked Meals (1 TP): ____
Drank & Tracked Daily Water Goal (1 TP): ____
Took a minimum of 3 Movement Breaks (1 TP): ____
Completed All 4 Daily Hygiene Activities (1 TP): ____
Wrote at least 2 Achievements & 2 Gratitudes (1 TP): ____

DAILY TOTAL: _____

Daily Quest Log

TODAY'S QUEST

Date:

TODAY'S QUEST TASKS

SIDE QUESTS

ALLIES & PARTY MEMBERS

QUEST JOURNAL

QUEST FINANCIALS

Daily Stats Log

MEALS & MOVEMENT PLANNER

YOUR STATS

WATER INTAKE:

MOVEMENT BREAKS:

SLEEP RATING: 1 2 3 4 5 **HOURS:** _____

NOTES:

MOOD:

HYGIENE:

OTHER:

NOTES, ACHIEVEMENTS & GRATITUDES

_____

_____

_____

_____

_____

REWARD CENTER

When you complete quest and journal items you receive TP. TP is used towards rewards in the Treasure Room!
Be sure to add up your points daily!

Completed Daily Objective (2 TP): ____
Completed 3 or More Quest Tasks (3 TP): ____
Planned & Tracked Meals (1 TP): ____
Drank & Tracked Daily Water Goal (1 TP): ____
Took a minimum of 3 Movement Breaks (1 TP): ____
Completed All 4 Daily Hygiene Activities (1 TP): ____
Wrote at least 2 Achievements & 2 Gratitudes (1 TP): ____

DAILY TOTAL: _____

Daily Quest Log

Date:

TODAY'S QUEST TASKS

SIDE QUESTS

ALLIES & PARTY MEMBERS

QUEST JOURNAL

QUEST FINANCIALS

Daily Stats Log

MEALS & MOVEMENT PLANNER

YOUR STATS

WATER INTAKE:

MOVEMENT BREAKS:

SLEEP RATING: 1 2 3 4 5 **HOURS:** _____

NOTES:

MOOD:

HYGIENE:

OTHER:

NOTES, ACHIEVEMENTS & GRATITUDES

_____
_____
_____
_____
_____

REWARD CENTER

When you complete quest and journal items you receive TP. TP is used towards rewards in the Treasure Room!
Be sure to add up your points daily!

Completed Daily Objective (2 TP): ____
Completed 3 or More Quest Tasks (3 TP): ____
Planned & Tracked Meals (1 TP): ____
Drank & Tracked Daily Water Goal (1 TP): ____
Took a minimum of 3 Movement Breaks (1 TP): ____
Completed All 4 Daily Hygiene Activities (1 TP): ____
Wrote at least 2 Achievements & 2 Gratitudes (1 TP): ____

DAILY TOTAL: _____

Daily Quest Log

TODAY'S QUEST

Date:

TODAY'S QUEST TASKS

SIDE QUESTS

ALLIES & PARTY MEMBERS

QUEST JOURNAL

QUEST FINANCIALS

Daily Stats Log

MEALS & MOVEMENT PLANNER

YOUR STATS

WATER INTAKE:

MOVEMENT BREAKS:

SLEEP RATING: HOURS:
1 2 3 4 5 _____

NOTES:

MOOD:

HYGIENE:

OTHER:

NOTES, ACHIEVEMENTS & GRATITUDES

_____
_____
_____
_____
_____

 REWARD CENTER

When you complete quest and journal items you receive TP. TP is used towards rewards in the Treasure Room!
Be sure to add up your points daily!

Completed Daily Objective (2 TP): ____
Completed 3 or More Quest Tasks (3 TP): ____
Planned & Tracked Meals (1 TP): ____
Drank & Tracked Daily Water Goal (1 TP): ____
Took a minimum of 3 Movement Breaks (1 TP): ____
Completed All 4 Daily Hygiene Activities (1 TP): ____
Wrote at least 2 Achievements & 2 Gratitudes (1 TP): ____

DAILY TOTAL: _____

Daily Quest Log

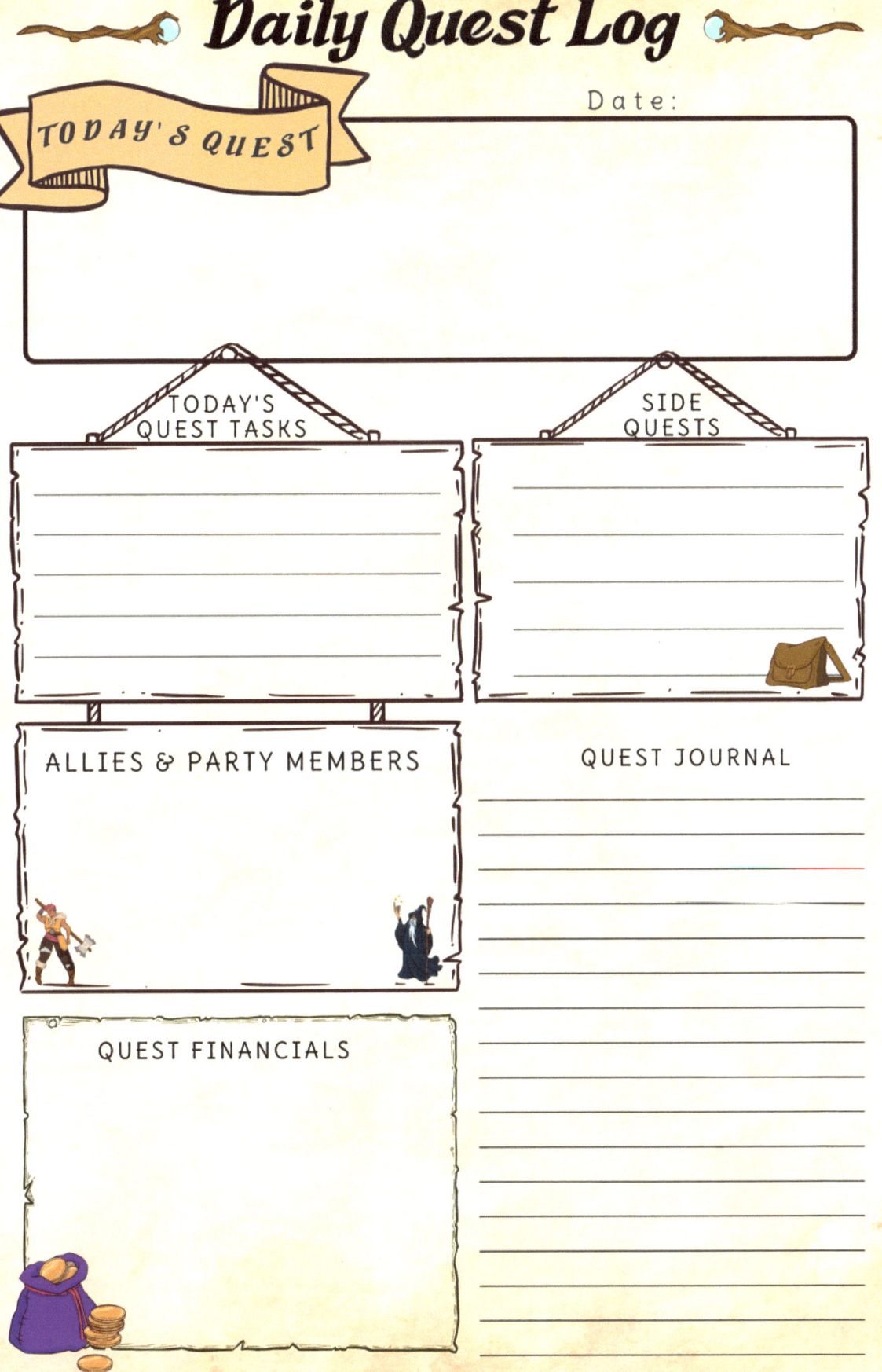

TODAY'S QUEST

Date:

TODAY'S QUEST TASKS

SIDE QUESTS

ALLIES & PARTY MEMBERS

QUEST JOURNAL

QUEST FINANCIALS

Daily Stats Log

MEALS & MOVEMENT PLANNER

YOUR STATS

WATER INTAKE:

MOVEMENT BREAKS:

SLEEP RATING: HOURS:
1 2 3 4 5   _ _ _ _ _

NOTES:

MOOD:

HYGIENE:

OTHER:

NOTES, ACHIEVEMENTS & GRATITUDES

_____

_____

_____

_____

_____

 ## REWARD CENTER

When you complete quest and journal items you receive TP. TP is used towards rewards in the Treasure Room!
Be sure to add up your points daily!

Completed Daily Objective (2 TP): ____
Completed 3 or More Quest Tasks (3 TP): ____
Planned & Tracked Meals (1 TP): ____
Drank & Tracked Daily Water Goal (1 TP): ____
Took a minimum of 3 Movement Breaks (1 TP): ____
Completed All 4 Daily Hygiene Activities (1 TP): ____
Wrote at least 2 Achievements & 2 Gratitudes (1 TP): ____

DAILY TOTAL: _____

Daily Quest Log

Date:

TODAY'S QUEST TASKS

SIDE QUESTS

ALLIES & PARTY MEMBERS

QUEST JOURNAL

QUEST FINANCIALS

Daily Stats Log

MEALS &
MOVEMENT PLANNER

YOUR STATS

WATER INTAKE:

MOVEMENT BREAKS:

SLEEP RATING: HOURS:
1 2 3 4 5 _____
NOTES:

MOOD:

HYGIENE:

OTHER:

NOTES , ACHIEVEMENTS & GRATITUDES

_____
_____
_____
_____
_____

 ## REWARD CENTER

When you complete quest and journal items you receive TP. TP is used towards rewards in the Treasure Room!
Be sure to add up your points daily!

Completed Daily Objective (2 TP): ____
Completed 3 or More Quest Tasks (3 TP): ____
Planned & Tracked Meals (1 TP): ____
Drank & Tracked Daily Water Goal (1 TP): ____
Took a minimum of 3 Movement Breaks (1 TP): ____
Completed All 4 Daily Hygiene Activities (1 TP): ____
Wrote at least 2 Achievements & 2 Gratitudes (1 TP): ____

DAILY TOTAL: _____

Daily Quest Log

Date:

TODAY'S QUEST TASKS

SIDE QUESTS

ALLIES & PARTY MEMBERS

QUEST JOURNAL

QUEST FINANCIALS

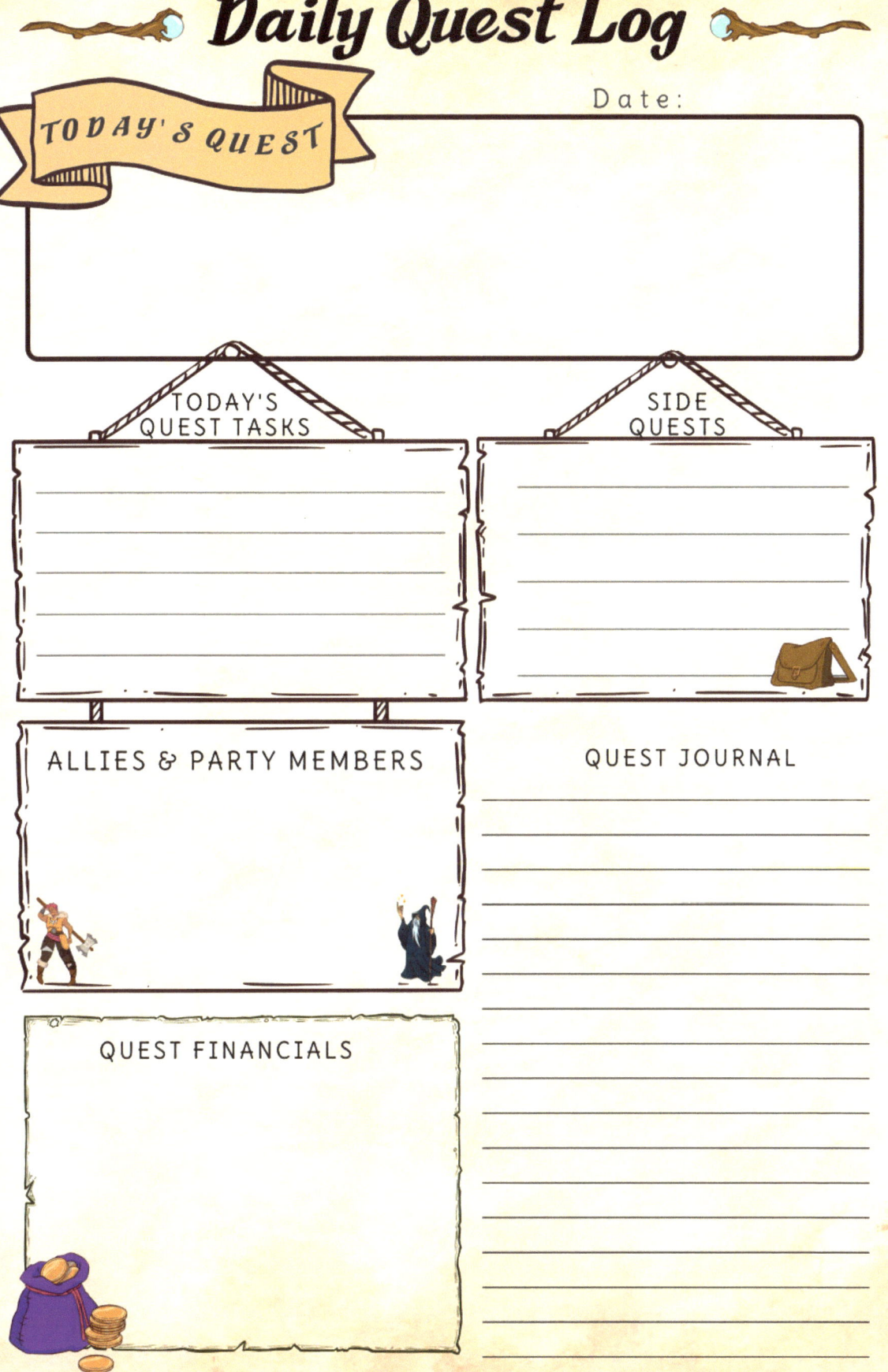

Daily Stats Log

**MEALS &
MOVEMENT PLANNER**

YOUR STATS

WATER INTAKE:

MOVEMENT BREAKS:

SLEEP RATING: **HOURS:**
Zzz...   1 2 3 4 5   _____
NOTES:

MOOD:

HYGIENE:

OTHER:

NOTES , ACHIEVEMENTS & GRATITUDES

_____

_____

_____

_____

_____

_____

 REWARD CENTER

When you complete quest and
journal items you receive TP.
TP is used towards rewards in
the Treasure Room!
Be sure to add up your points
daily!

Completed Daily Objective (2 TP): ____
Completed 3 or More Quest Tasks (3 TP): ____
Planned & Tracked Meals (1 TP): ____
Drank & Tracked Daily Water Goal (1 TP): ____
Took a minimum of 3 Movement Breaks (1 TP): ____
Completed All 4 Daily Hygiene Activities (1 TP): ____
Wrote at least 2 Achievements & 2 Gratitudes (1 TP): ____

DAILY TOTAL: _____

Daily Quest Log

TODAY'S QUEST

Date:

TODAY'S QUEST TASKS

SIDE QUESTS

ALLIES & PARTY MEMBERS

QUEST JOURNAL

QUEST FINANCIALS

Leisure Planner

DATE(S) _____

LEISURE ACTIVITES

INVITATION LIST

EVENT DETAILS

LOCATION:

TIME/DURATION:

THEME:

REMIND GUESTS TO BRING

MENU & BEVERAGES

NOTES

_____
_____
_____
_____
_____
_____
_____

Weekly Check In

WEEK OF _____

REWARD CENTER WEEKLY TOTALS

Monday _____
Tuesday _____
Wednesday _____
Thursday _____
Friday _____
Saturday _____
Sunday _____
Bonus 1 _____
Bonus 2 _____

WEEKLY TOTAL: _____

ROLLING TOTAL: _____

PARTY MEMBERS & ALLIES TO THANK THIS WEEK

MONSTERS BEATEN THIS WEEK

NOTES, ACHIEVEMENTS AND GRATITUDES FOR THE WEEK

_____
_____
_____
_____
_____
_____
_____
_____
_____
_____
_____
_____
_____
_____
_____
_____
_____
_____
_____
_____
_____
_____

Journal

Journal

Journal

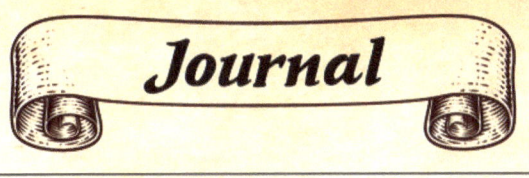

Journal

Congratulations Adventuerer!

You have completed another segment of your journey toward achieving your vision of your best life.

You have traveled a great distance. You have conquered so many monsters. And you have grown as an Adventurer just by taking on and completing this part of the journey.

Your Quest may be complete or it may not. You may have a long way to go or just a few more weeks. Either way, you should be proud of yourself, for the journey is the true destination and the results are the reward.

I hope you continue to journey with us.
It has been my honor to serve as your guide.

Happy Questing!

- *Selina Belle*

"Every Quest must contain several key elements. And a dragon. No good quest is complete without a dragon."

Happy Questing!

- Selina Belle

Selina Belle is a lifestyle coach for gamers who decided to marry 20 years of entrepreneurship and business coaching experience with her passion for having fun, playing video games, and creative writing. She's on a mission to bring the engaging power of gaming into the real world to support gamers in their businesses, careers and personal lives. She believes that we are all the designers of our own futures and the heroes of our own Quests.

www.ingramcontent.com/pod-product-compliance
Lightning Source LLC
Chambersburg PA
CBHW041615120626
46551CB00003B/454